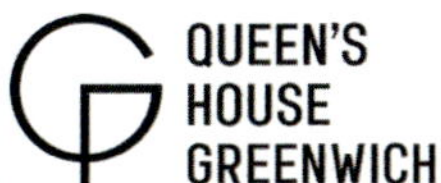

SPOTLIGHT SERIES

J.M.W. Turner's *The Battle of Trafalgar*

Commemoration and Controversy

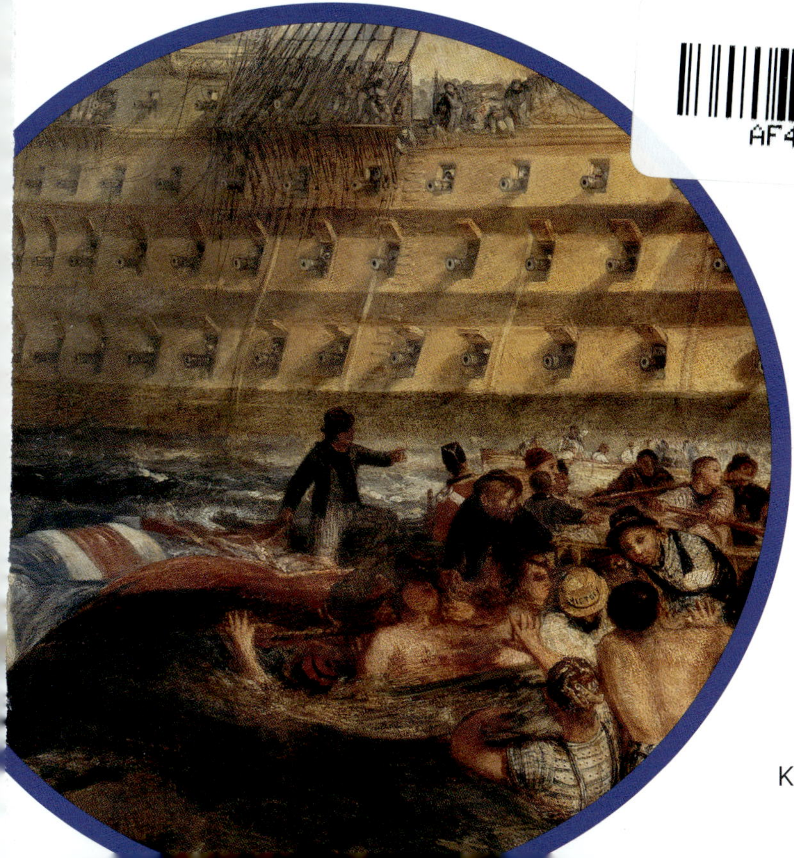

Katherine Gazzard

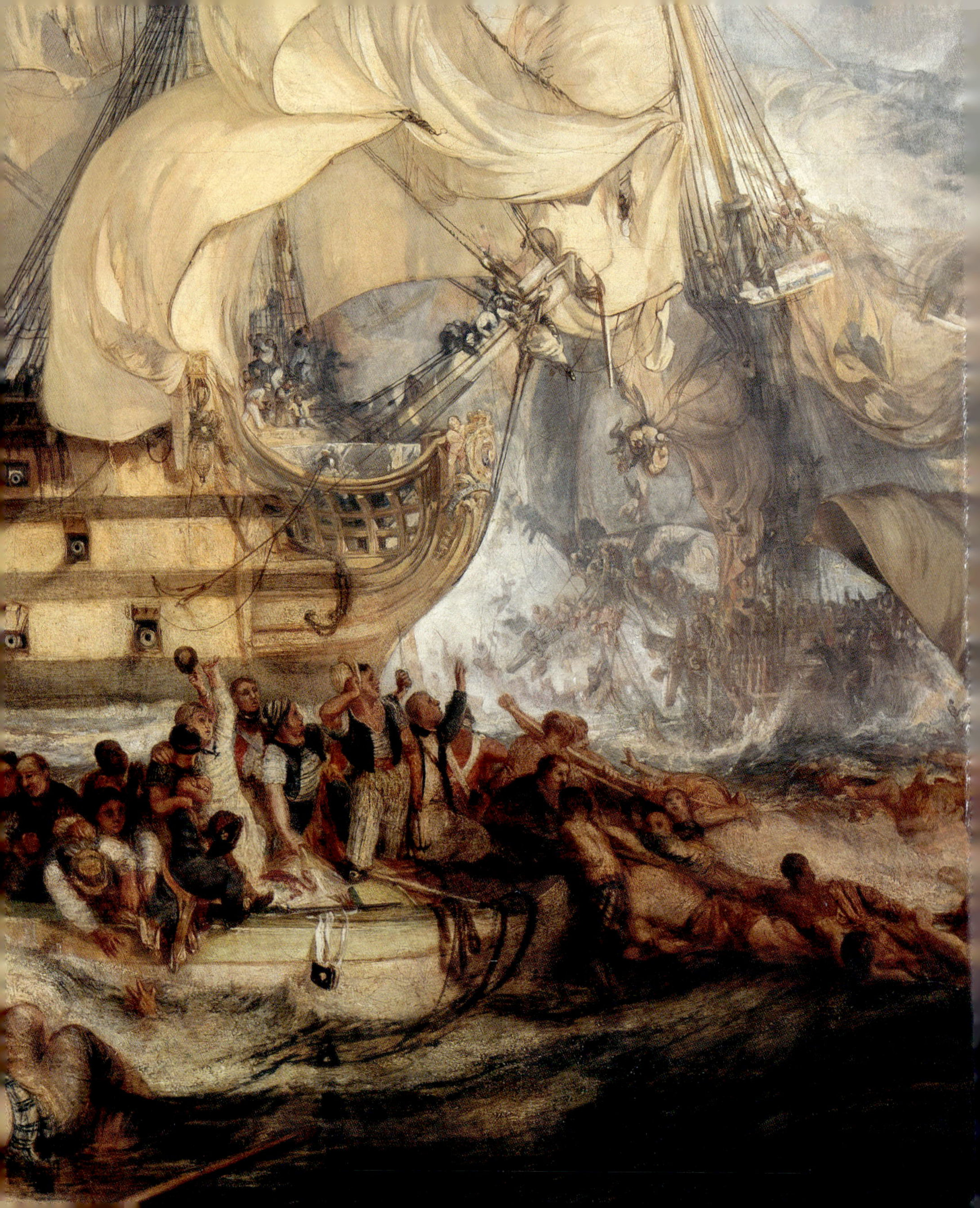

Contents

FIG. 1
The Battle of Trafalgar,
J.M.W. Turner,
1822–24,
oil on canvas,
2,615 × 3,685mm,
BHC0565

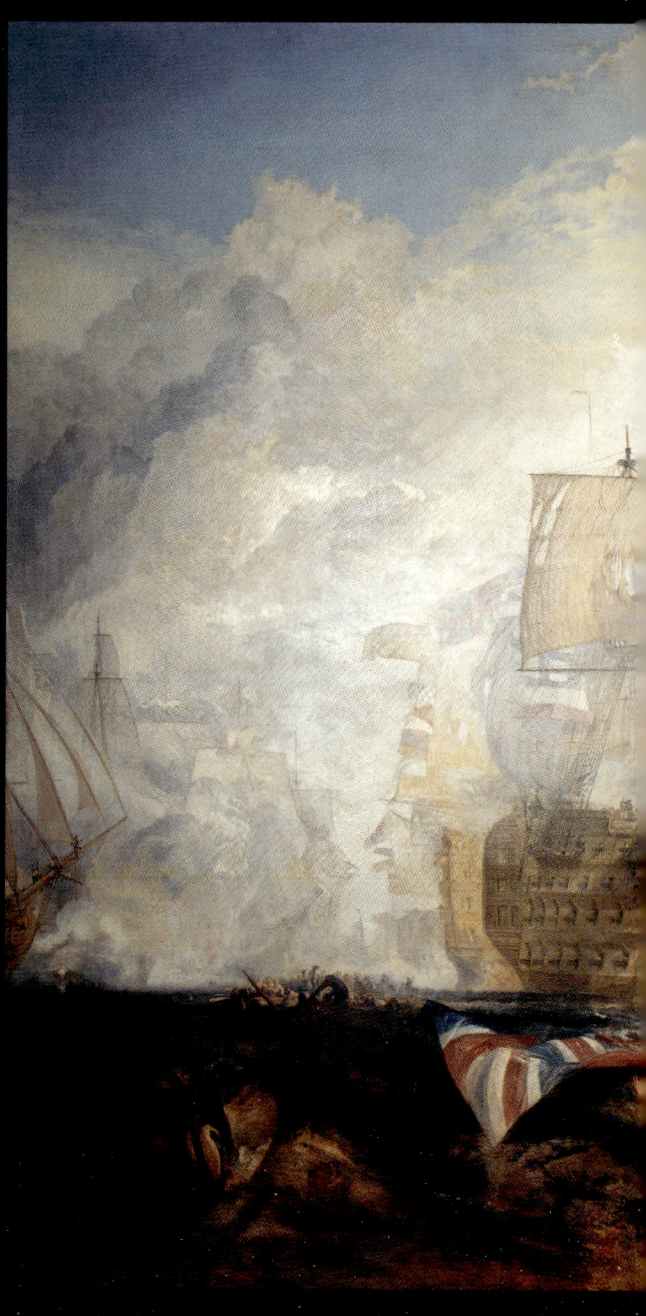

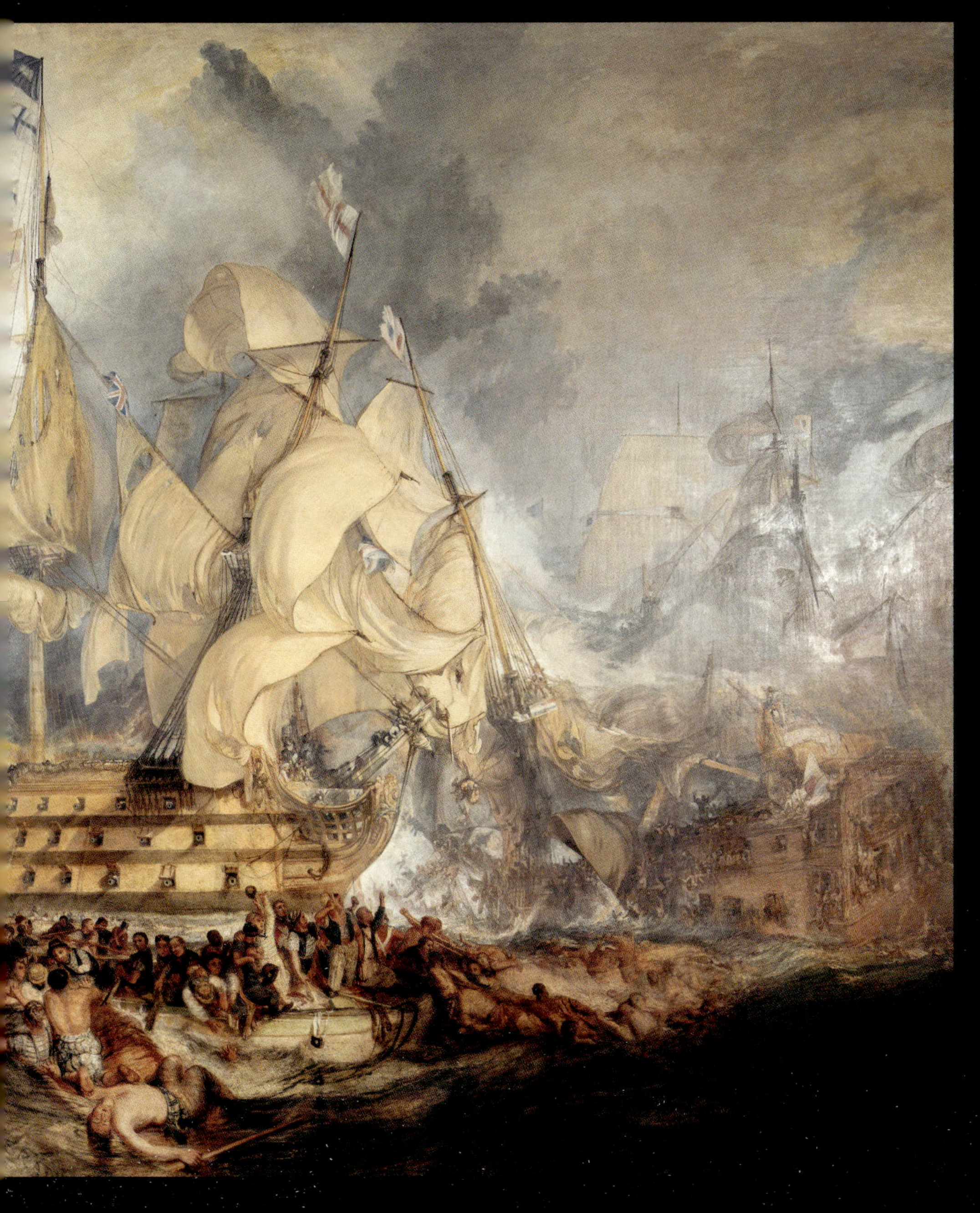

Chapter 1
The Artist and the Battle

Joseph Mallord William Turner (1775–1851) is one of Britain's most celebrated artists and *The Battle of Trafalgar* should be regarded as among his most important paintings (fig. 1). Measuring over three metres wide and two metres tall (over 11 by 8ft), it is the largest painting that he ever completed. It also has the unique distinction of being his only royal commission, having been made for King George IV (reigned 1820–30). Furthermore, it depicts a historically and nationally significant event, showing the victory of the British Royal Navy over a combined French and Spanish fleet off Cape Trafalgar on 21 October 1805 in what is widely regarded as the most decisive naval action of the Napoleonic Wars.

However, for all its apparent importance, art historians do not often write about the painting, except to comment on the storm of criticism that followed its unveiling at St James's Palace in 1824. The harshest critics were naval officers, who objected to historical inaccuracies in Turner's representation of the battle. Their opprobrium continued to overshadow the painting after George IV donated it to the National Gallery of Naval Art (known as the Naval Gallery) at Greenwich Hospital in 1829. Some observers interpreted the donation as an act of royal rejection, proving that the King himself was dissatisfied with the picture. To this day, *The Battle of Trafalgar* is less celebrated than some of Turner's other works. It has gained an unfortunate reputation as something of a failure.

Yet it is important to look beyond the negative comments that have haunted the painting since its creation. *The Battle of Trafalgar* is a complex and sophisticated artwork, which weaves together conventions from several artistic genres. It combines a celebration of maritime victory with a tribute to a national hero, an ode to ordinary sailors and a meditation on the horrors of war. If Turner failed to represent the facts of the battle, it was because he was trying to encapsulate its immense significance within the British cultural imagination. Moreover, the painting's move to Greenwich was by no means an ignominious fate. It marked the culmination of George IV's enthusiastic patronage of the Naval Gallery and turned *The Battle of Trafalgar* into the centrepiece of a popular public art gallery located at the heart of a naval institution, where retired and disabled veterans were housed and supported. Since its transfer from Greenwich Hospital to the National Maritime Museum on long-term loan in 1936, the painting has been a major highlight of the Museum's collection. This book unpacks the history and significance of the masterpiece, starting with the stories of its creator and of the battle that it depicts.

The artist

Turner, who was known as William to his friends and family, was born in Covent Garden, London, in 1775 and baptised on 14 May that year. His precise date of birth is uncertain. In later life, he claimed to have been born on Saint George's Day (23 April), which was also the supposed birthday of William Shakespeare. However, this assertion has never been verified. It may have been a creative fiction that Turner cultivated, ambitiously seeking to place himself in the pantheon of national treasures through association with England's patron saint and its most famous playwright.

At a time when most artists came from middle-class families, he proudly emphasised his humble origins. The son of a barber, he kept his Cockney accent throughout his life. His interest in art developed at an early age and, from the start, he seems to have found inspiration in the sea. Turner's earliest surviving watercolours depict the coastal town of Margate in Kent, where he went to stay with one of his mother's relatives in the summer of 1786. He was admitted as a student at the Royal Academy Schools in December 1789, where he learnt to draw plaster casts of ancient sculptures before progressing to life-drawing classes. The Academy's curriculum focused on the representation of the human figure, which was regarded as the pinnacle of artistic achievement. Genres that did not involve human subject matter, such as landscape and still life, were ignored, but Turner taught himself the art of landscape drawing in his own time.

Turner began showing drawings and watercolours at the Royal Academy's annual exhibitions in 1790. Six years later, he exhibited his first oil painting, a moonlight view of small boats off the Isle of Wight entitled *Fishermen at Sea* (fig. 2). At this time, paintings were considered more prestigious than drawings, hence the exhibition of *Fishermen at Sea* was a landmark moment in Turner's career, effectively announcing his arrival as a mature artist. His choice of a seafaring scene for his debut painting highlighted his particular interest in maritime subjects, which would continue throughout his career.

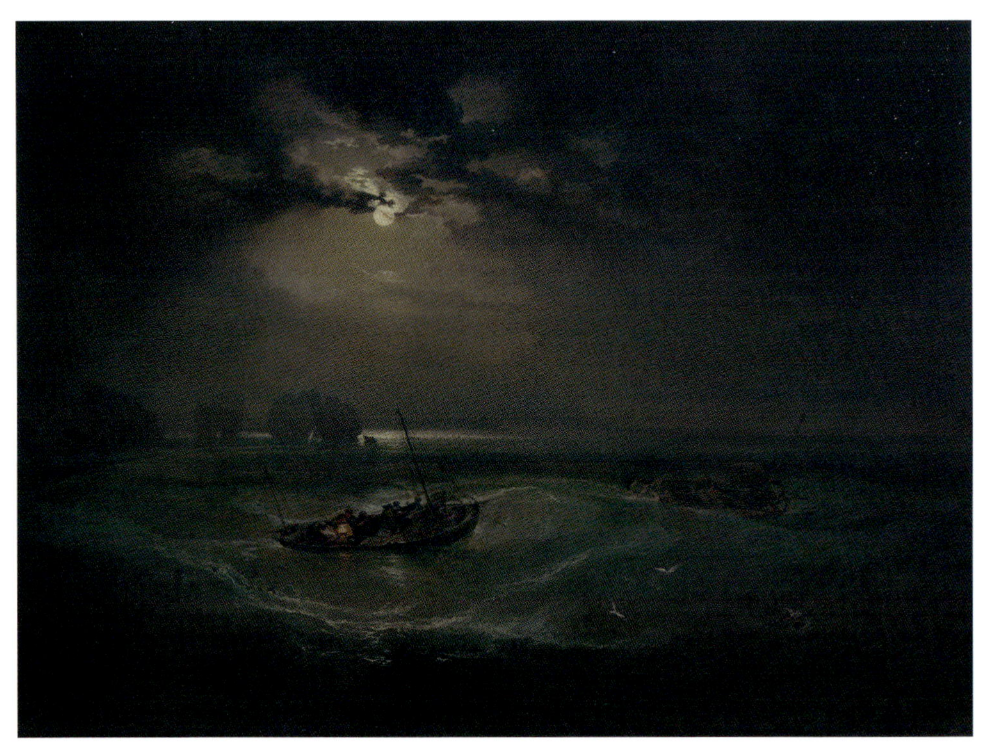

FIG. 2
Fishermen at Sea,
J.M.W. Turner,
1796,
oil on canvas,
914 × 1,222mm,
Tate

Turner's work demonstrates his fascination with both the sea itself and also the art of marine painting, a genre dedicated to the representation of ships and naval battles. Given his lowly social background, he had few opportunities during his youth to see major art collections. However, he developed his art historical knowledge through the study of engravings, mezzotints and other prints, which provided an affordable means of accessing famous paintings. As an older man, Turner is said to have told a friend that one print in particular had inspired him. 'This,' he said, 'made me a painter.' The print in question was an image of a ship in a gale, printed in blue-green ink, from a series of mezzotints based on paintings by the Dutch artist Willem van de Velde the Younger (1633–1707, fig. 3).

Marine painting developed in the Dutch Republic in the late sixteenth and early seventeenth centuries. The genre was grounded in realism, with artists striving to produce convincing representations of ships and fleets. Yet, under the pretence of accuracy, the imagery of hulls, masts, yards, sails, rigging and flags conveyed symbolic meanings, from the glorification of overseas trade to the promotion of naval might. This artistic tradition subsequently took root in Britain, its popularity growing in tandem with the nation's rise as a global maritime power. Van de Velde the Younger – whose work Turner later acknowledged as an inspiration – had a profound impact on

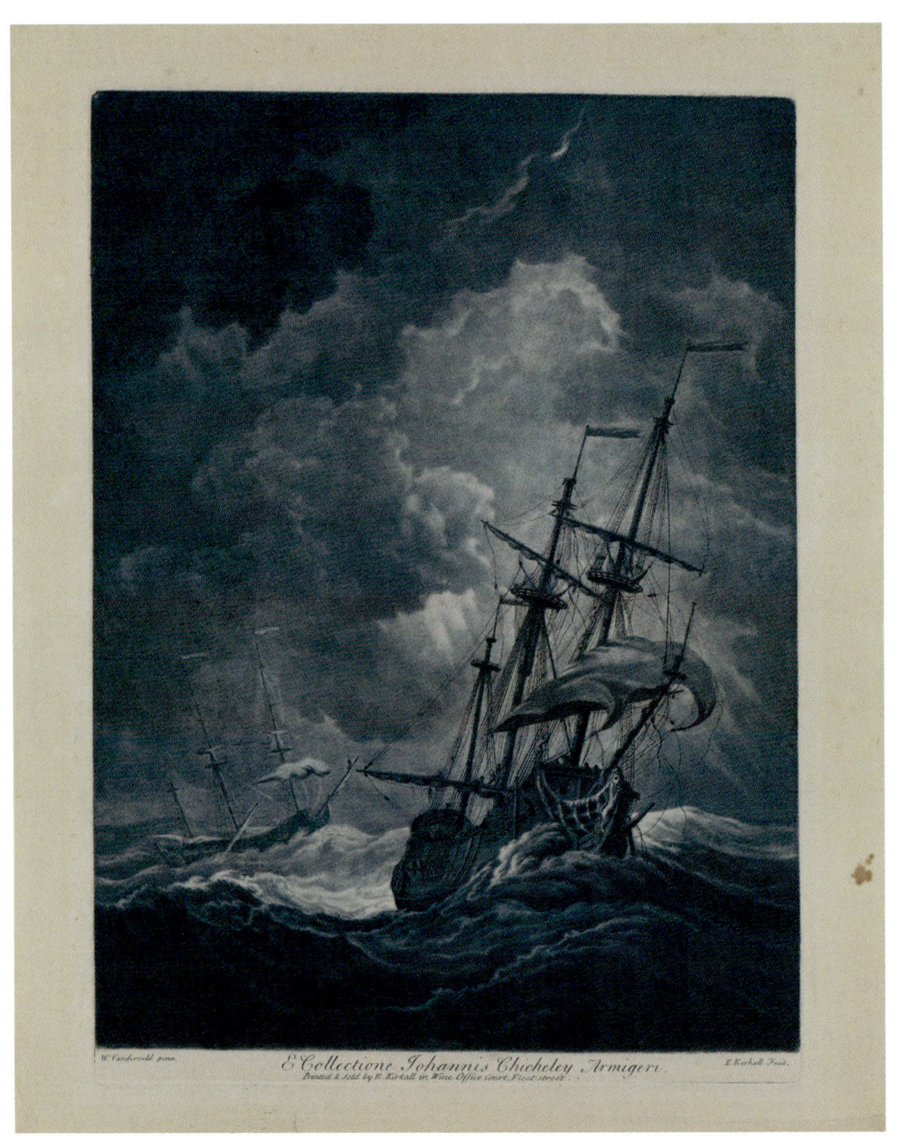
W Vandevelde pinx.
E Collectione Johannis Chicheley Armigeri.
Printed & Sold by E. Kirkall in Wine Office Court, Fleet street.
E Kirkall Fecit.

the development of British marine painting. He moved from Amsterdam to London with his father in 1672 and established a family studio at the Queen's House in Greenwich. His influence is reflected in many of Turner's paintings.

The practice of marine painting was usually a niche specialism. Most marine painters were dedicated to the genre, immersing themselves in technical details of ship design and fleet manoeuvres in order to appeal to an expert audience of naval officers and enthusiasts. Turner, by contrast, pursued a more varied career path. As well as seascapes, he painted landscapes and historical scenes, subjects which held greater prestige within the art world. He also tended to employ poetic licence in his maritime works, rather than adhering to the exacting approach that other marine painters favoured. Yet the representation of the sea nevertheless remained central to his artistic identity. He even adopted a maritime alter-ego, calling himself 'Admiral Booth' after moving to Chelsea in 1846 with Sophia Caroline Booth, a widow with whom he had a romantic relationship. His assumption of this seafaring persona suggests that he felt an affinity with naval officers.

Turner's career progressed quickly following the exhibition of *Fishermen at Sea*. In 1799, aged only 24, he was elected an Associate of the Royal Academy. Three years later, he became a full Academician and, between 1807 and 1837,

FIG. 3 *A Ship Scudding in a Gale*, Elisha Kirkall after Willem van de Velde the Younger, about 1725–30, mezzotint printed in colour, 433 × 309mm, PAG6881

he served as the Academy's Professor of Perspective. His involvement with the Royal Academy reveals his respect for tradition and his desire for official recognition from Britain's artistic establishment. Yet Turner also honed his reputation as an outsider and an innovator. He disregarded creative conventions and embraced the subject matter of the modern world, from current events and new technologies to social change and the growth of industry. This strand within his practice culminated in late works like *Snow Storm – Steam-Boat off a Harbour's Mouth*, which was exhibited in 1842 (fig. 4). Decried at the time as 'soapsuds and whitewash', the painting's whirling vortex of light and shadow anticipated impressionism and other avant-garde art movements of the later nineteenth century.

Turner was thus a complex and sometimes contradictory artist. He found inspiration in seafaring subjects but distanced himself from specialist marine painters. He craved traditional honours but often produced shockingly unconventional artworks. *The Battle of Trafalgar* shines a spotlight on these dichotomies. Coming from the King, the commission was a prestigious accolade, but Turner's unorthodox composition caused public controversy. He was personally fascinated by the subject matter, but representing one of the most famous naval events in British history was not a straightforward task.

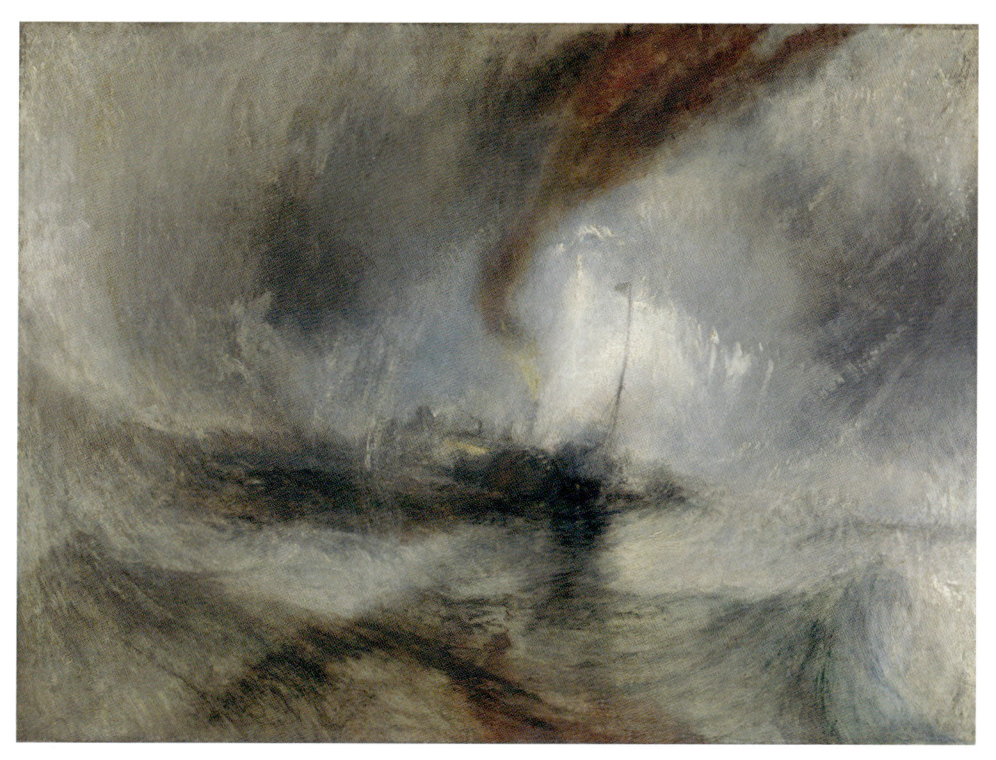

FIG. 4
Snow Storm – Steam-Boat off a Harbour's Mouth,
J.M.W. Turner,
1842,
oil on canvas,
914 × 1,219mm,
Tate

The battle

Turner's emergence as an artist coincided with a period of global upheaval. In the same year that he started attending the Royal Academy Schools, the French Revolution sent shockwaves through Europe, leading to a series of sweeping military conflicts around the world. From the declaration of war in January 1793 to the final defeat of Napoleon Bonaparte (1769–1821) at the Battle of Waterloo in June 1815, Britain and France were locked in a prolonged struggle for military, naval and imperial supremacy. This conflict had a profound effect on British art. Visiting Italy to study Renaissance masterpieces had historically been a rite of passage for British artists, but the hostilities restricted European travel. Instead, artists turned to the culture and landscapes of their home nation for creative inspiration. Some artists engaged directly with the war effort, electing to paint patriotic subjects, military portraits and battle scenes. Others highlighted the political tensions and tragic loss of life that accompanied the conflict.

The Battle of Trafalgar was a defining moment in the war and inspired many artistic responses. The action took place on 21 October 1805, off Cape Trafalgar on Spain's south-west coast. The British were outnumbered by their French and Spanish opponents, having only 27 ships-of-the-line compared to the allied fleet's 33. To overcome this numerical disadvantage, the British commander, Vice-Admiral Lord Horatio Nelson (1758–1805), employed a risky tactical approach. Rather than forming a line parallel with the opposing fleet, which was a traditional method for fighting naval battles, he split his ships into two columns and ordered them to sail directly at the enemy. This was dangerous because it meant the foremost British ships were sailing head-on into broadsides from French and Spanish guns. Eventually, however, the two British columns reached the allied fleet and broke through its line, delivering devastating fire as soon as they got in among the enemy ships. The battle splintered into a brutal melee, from which the British emerged victorious. Twenty-one allied ships were captured, and one was destroyed. Over 4,000 French and Spanish sailors lost their lives. The British did not lose any ships, but 456 individuals were killed, including Nelson himself, who died from a bullet wound. The fatal shot came from a sniper positioned at the top of the mizzen (rear) mast on the French ship *Redoutable*.

Britain's victory at Trafalgar did not end the war. Napoleon's conquest of the European mainland proceeded unabated. Fighting also continued at sea, but the Royal Navy had at least gained a significant advantage over its diminished opponents. The public perception at the time was that the battle had emphatically proved Britain's naval superiority. There was a long tradition of celebrating maritime success within British culture, stretching back to the widespread public commemorations that followed the defeat of the Spanish Armada in 1588. Britain's national identity was bound up with the idea of naval supremacy.

Nelson's death further enhanced Trafalgar's cultural impact. Before the battle, he was already a celebrated, albeit complex, public figure. He was garlanded with titles and other official accolades. At the same time, he was popular with common sailors and ordinary people, inspiring among the disenfranchised lower classes a level of enthusiasm that alarmed the ruling elite. Society gossip swirled around his colourful private life, most notably his affair with Emma Hamilton (1765–1815). At sea, his self-aggrandisement and relentless pursuit of glory both pleased and frustrated his naval superiors. Some regarded his tactical emphasis on inflicting maximum destruction as risky and irresponsible. For others, it was proof of his visionary genius. Nelson and Turner never met, although they were arguably kindred spirits: both longed to be respected as national heroes but they also embodied maverick tendencies.

By losing his life in his greatest victory, Nelson sealed his status as a legendary figure in British naval history. 'If ever there were a hero who merited the honours of a public funeral, and a public mourning,' declared *The Times* newspaper at the time, 'it is the pious, the modest, and the gallant Nelson, the darling of the British navy, whose death has plunged the whole nation into the deepest grief; and to whose talents and bravery, even the enemy he has conquered will bear testimony.' This rhetoric is typical of the coverage that surrounded Nelson's death.

The satirical printmaker James Gillray (1756–1815) took aim at the rush to apotheosise the late Vice-Admiral in an etching entitled *The Death of Admiral Lord Nelson in the moment of Victory* (fig. 5). This print was released by Gillray's publisher Hannah Humphrey on 23 December 1805, only two months after Trafalgar. It shows Nelson collapsing on the quarterdeck of his flagship, the *Victory*, into the arms of Britannia, a traditional personification of the British nation. Gillray has playfully given her the face and body of Emma Hamilton. King George III kneels at Nelson's side and two sailors present him with a captured French flag. The British flag flies in the background, inscribed 'Victory' in reference to the name of the ship and the outcome of the battle. Above, a winged embodiment of Fame blows a trumpet and inscribes the word 'Immortality' in the swirling smoke from the battle. Although less pointed than the majority of Gillray's caricatures, this imagery is designed to appear somewhat overblown and

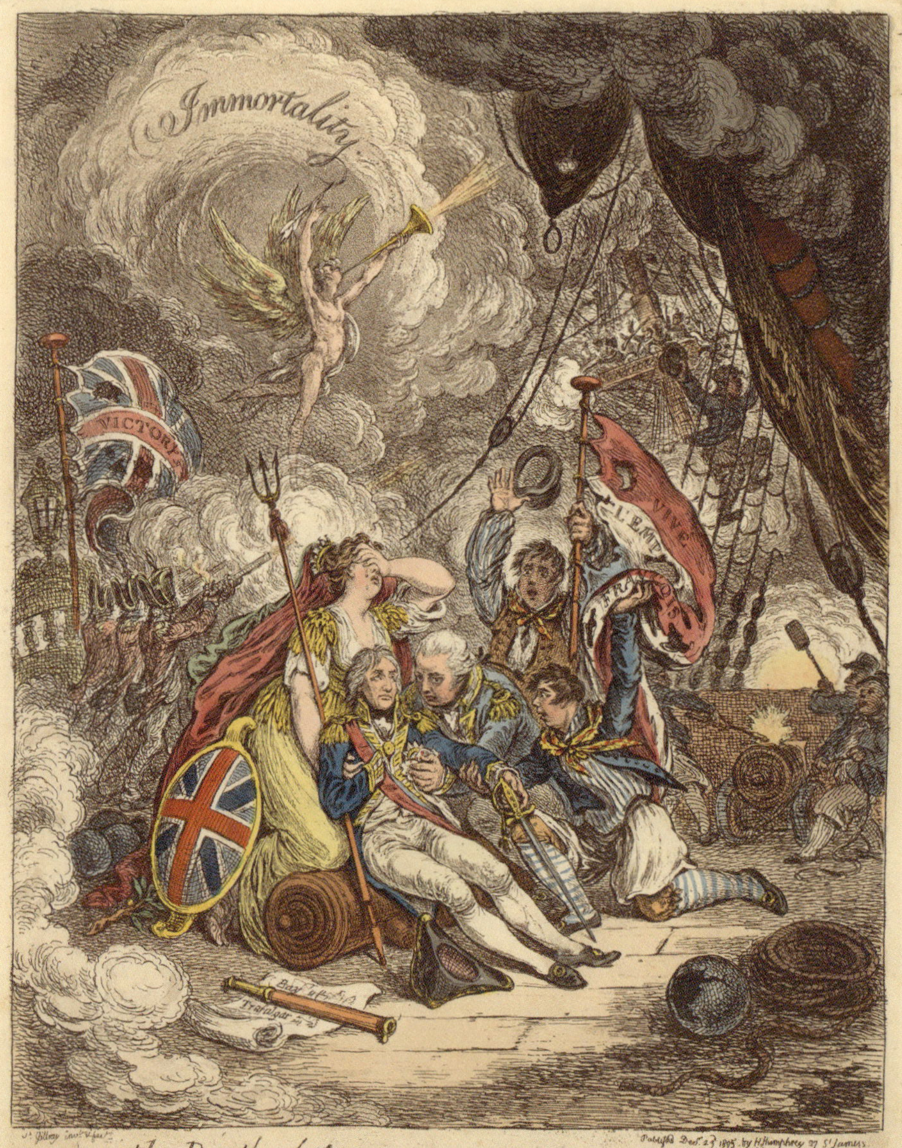

Js. Gillray inv. & fect.

Publish'd Decr. 23 1805 by H. Humphrey 27 St. James's

— the Death of ADMIRAL-LORD-NELSON, – in the moment of Victory! —

this Design for the Memorial intended by the City of London to commemorate the Glorious Death of the immortal Nelson, is with every sentiment of respect, humbly submitted to the Right honble. the Lord Mayor & the Court of Aldermen.

ridiculous, poking fun at the hyperbolic rhetoric that greeted Nelson's death.

While designed as a satire, *The Death of Admiral Lord Nelson* anticipated the numerous artistic representations of Nelson's fate that proliferated in the years that followed. As early as November 1805, the print publisher Josiah Boydell (1752–1817) had published a newspaper advertisement offering 500 guineas 'to a British artist to paint either the Battle of Trafalgar or the Death of Lord Nelson, from which a print will be produced'. Artists immediately began competing to claim the cash prize, which was worth more than the annual salary for a captain in the Royal Navy at the time.

In 1806, Benjamin West (1738–1820) unveiled his version of the subject in a special exhibition at his home and studio in Westminster. West was one of Britain's leading artists at this time, having served as the President of the Royal Academy of Arts since 1792. He briefly stood down from this role in late 1805 but was re-elected to the post the following year. The setting for his painting *The Death of Nelson* is the quarterdeck of the *Victory* (fig. 6). Nelson lies in the centre, surrounded by his officers. The ship's company gather around, one of the sailors coming forward to present a surrendered Spanish flag to the Vice-Admiral as a trophy. Although the composition is

FIG. 5 *The Death of Admiral Lord Nelson in the moment of Victory*, James Gillray, 1805, hand-coloured etching on paper, 409 × 299mm, PAF3866

FIG. 6
The Death of Nelson,
Benjamin West,
1806,
oil on canvas,
1,822 × 2,476mm,
National Museums Liverpool

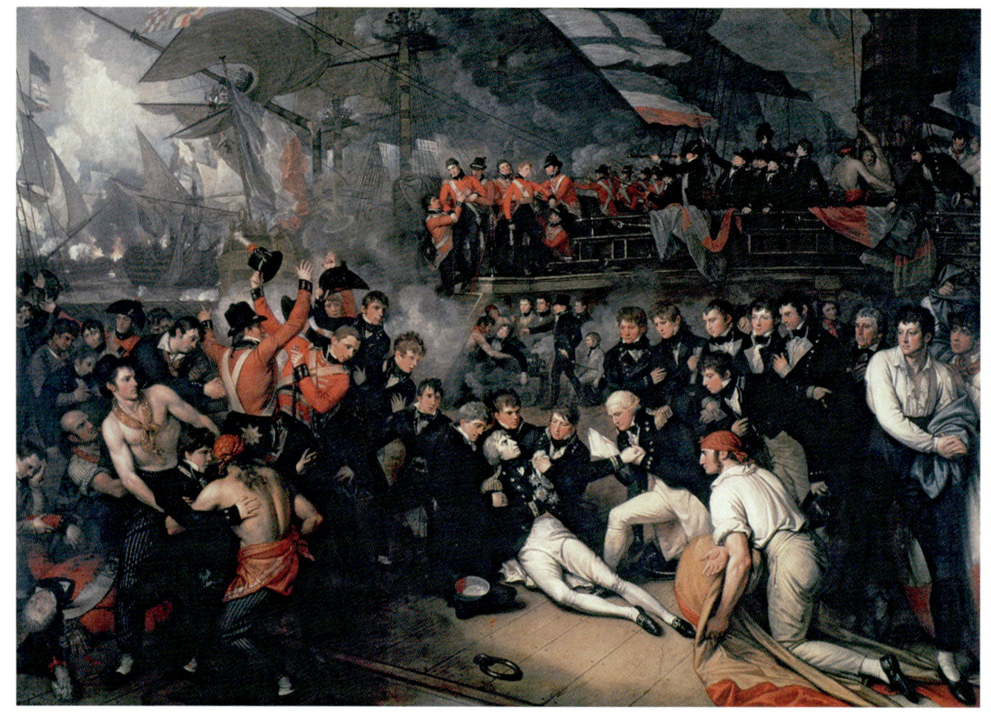

reminiscent of Gillray's satirical take on the subject, the tone here is entirely serious.

Given his preeminent status in the art world, West seems to have taken for granted that he would win Boydell's prize. He therefore felt aggrieved when Boydell awarded the 500 guineas to Arthur William Devis (1762–1822), a struggling painter who had recently spent time in debtors' prison. Devis had obtained special permission from his gaolers to travel from London to Portsmouth to meet the *Victory* when it returned from Trafalgar with Nelson's body on board. He then befriended the ship's officers and gained an invitation to go aboard. As the *Victory* sailed round the coast to the mouth of the Thames Estuary, Devis interviewed witnesses to Nelson's death, made sketches of the ship and even witnessed the Vice-Admiral's autopsy.

This factual research underpins his painting (fig. 7). The setting is the cockpit, a cramped space in the bowels of the ship where the surgeon was stationed during a battle. Nelson had been taken to the cockpit after being shot. He was still alive at that time but succumbed to his injuries about three hours later. In Devis's painting, the Vice-Admiral has been stripped of his uniform, which lies discarded in the foreground. The scene is idealised, evoking Renaissance paintings of the lamentation of Christ, but it is closer to the reality of Nelson's death than West's treatment of the subject.

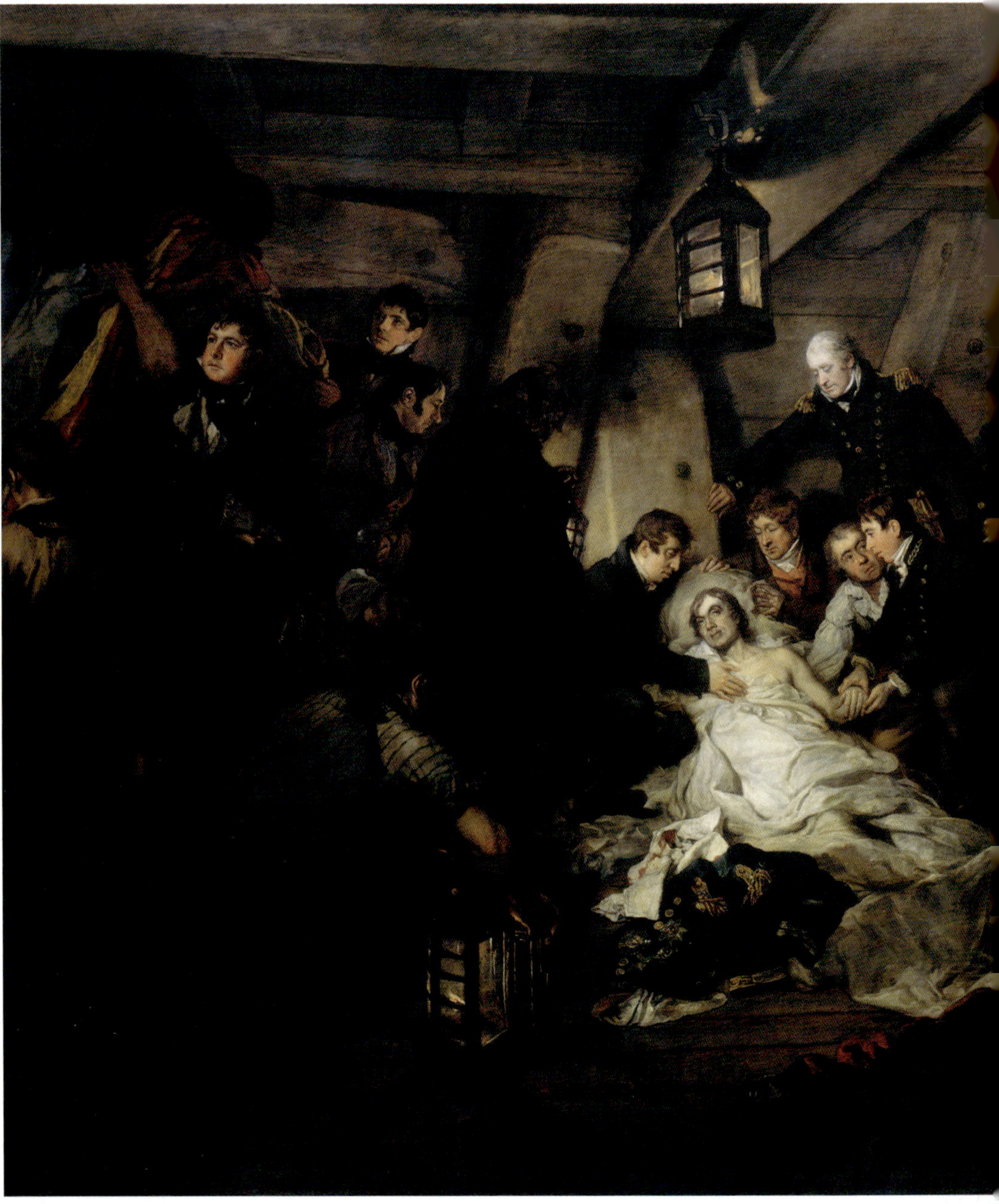

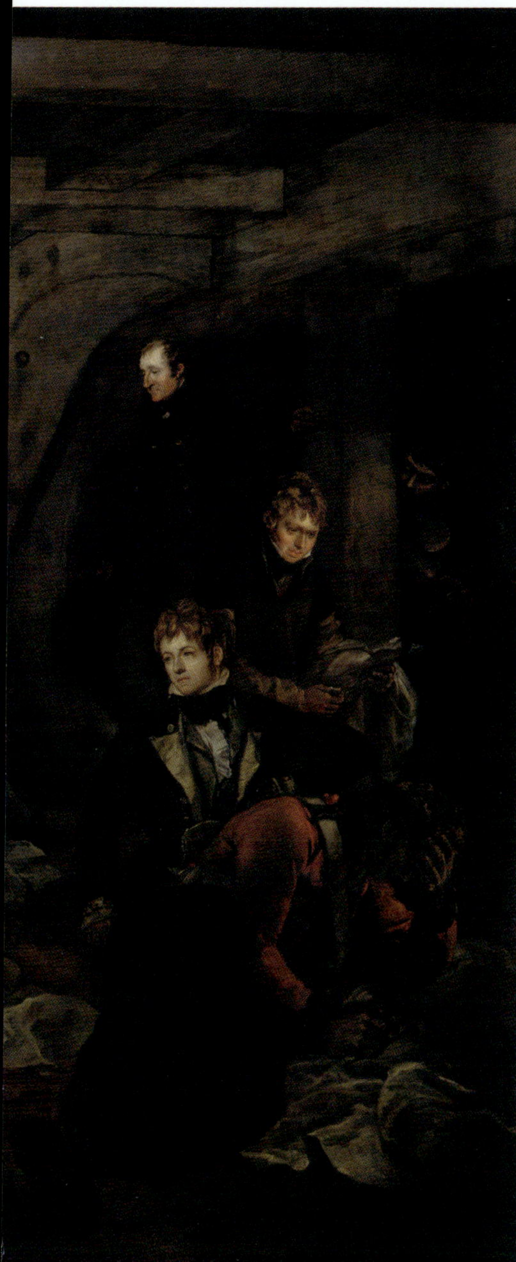

FIG. 7
The Death of Nelson,
Arthur William Devis,
1807,
oil on canvas,
1,956 × 2,616mm,
BHC2894

West defended his decision to show Nelson's death on the quarterdeck on the grounds that this made for an 'epic composition' and was more appropriate to the 'dignity and high importance' of the event. By contrast, he declared of Devis's painting that 'no boy would be animated by a representation of Nelson dying like an ordinary man' in the 'gloomy hold of a ship'. These comments are indicative of West's wounded pride, but they also reflect a broader debate within British art at this time. The question at its heart was whether, when representing important historical moments, artists should prioritise epic grandeur over factual accuracy, or vice versa. One school of thought was that the ideas and emotions conveyed in a picture were more important than the specifics of the scene. This viewpoint was championed by the Royal Academy, but it found little traction beyond the inner circles of the art world. Many viewers and critics preferred paintings that offered literal interpretations of their subjects. The debate was still ongoing two decades later when Turner's *The Battle of Trafalgar* was completed. Much of the criticism directed at the painting condemned Turner's decision to deviate from the facts of the action to create a more epic expression of the battle's significance.

Turner's fascination with Trafalgar had begun in the immediate aftermath of the event. While West and Devis were working on their paintings in late 1805, he was creating one of his own. Like Devis, he undertook first-hand research, sketching the *Victory* as it entered the Medway and making detailed studies on board while it was refitting at Chatham Dockyard. In one sketch, Turner noted where guns had been positioned during the action and where splinters had struck the deck rail (fig. 8).

His research culminated in *The Battle of Trafalgar, as Seen from the Mizen Starboard Shrouds of the 'Victory'*, which he revealed to the public in June 1806 at his studio-gallery in Queen Anne Street, London (fig. 9). The painting depicts the moments following Nelson's wounding. Marines and sailors prepare to carry the injured Vice-Admiral below deck, while a group of their shipmates watch on with a captured French flag. These elements echo West's *The Death of Nelson*, but Turner adopts a different viewpoint. In his version of the scene, the action on the quarterdeck is small and distant, as it would have appeared to the sailors scrambling up and down the *Victory*'s rigging. This elevated viewpoint allowed Turner to combine the human drama of Nelson's fate with the ship-to-ship fighting of the wider battle. The background is a jumble of hulls, masts and gun smoke, evoking the chaos that Nelson's aggressive tactics had induced.

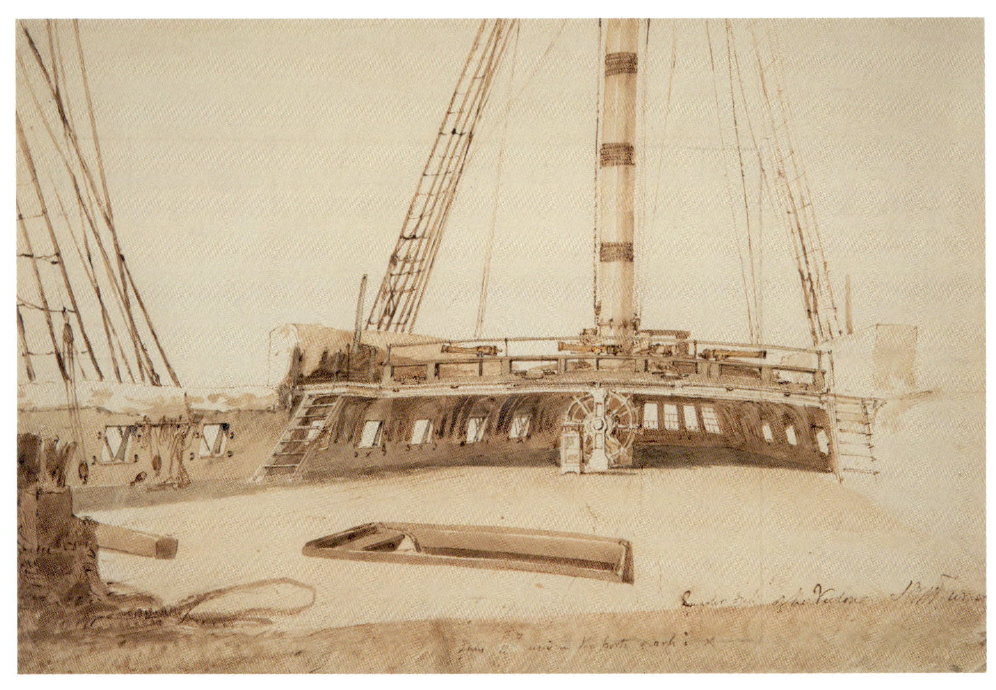

FIG. 8
The 'Victory': From Quarterdeck to Poop,
J.M.W. Turner,
1805,
pen and ink, graphite and watercolour on paper,
424 × 565mm,
Tate

Initial viewers of the painting complained that it appeared unfinished. Turner therefore continued to work on the picture over the next two years. When he exhibited it again at the British Institution for Promoting the Fine Arts in 1808, the response was more favourable. One reviewer called it 'a British epic picture [...] the first picture of the kind that has ever, to our knowledge been exhibited'. 'Mr. Turner,' the critic explained, 'has detailed the death of his hero, while he has suggested the whole of a great naval victory, which we believe has never before been successfully accomplished [...] in a single picture.' These comments present the painting as unique and original, reinforcing Turner's reputation as an innovative artist. He is described as depicting the death of 'his hero', implying that the picture is a personal response to Nelson's fate. The painting certainly stemmed from Turner's interest in the subject. It had not been produced for a particular patron, and it remained in the artist's own collection until his death.

Almost two decades later, Turner returned to the subject of Trafalgar. This time, however, he was working for King George IV. Intended for a royal palace, his painting had to meet particular requirements in terms of its size and composition. No longer a recent event, Trafalgar had by now acquired the status of a modern legend. Encapsulating its significance would test Turner's ingenuity to the limit.

FIG. 9
The Battle of Trafalgar, as Seen from the Mizen Starboard Shrouds of the 'Victory', J.M.W. Turner, 1806–08, oil on canvas, 1,708 × 2,388mm, Tate

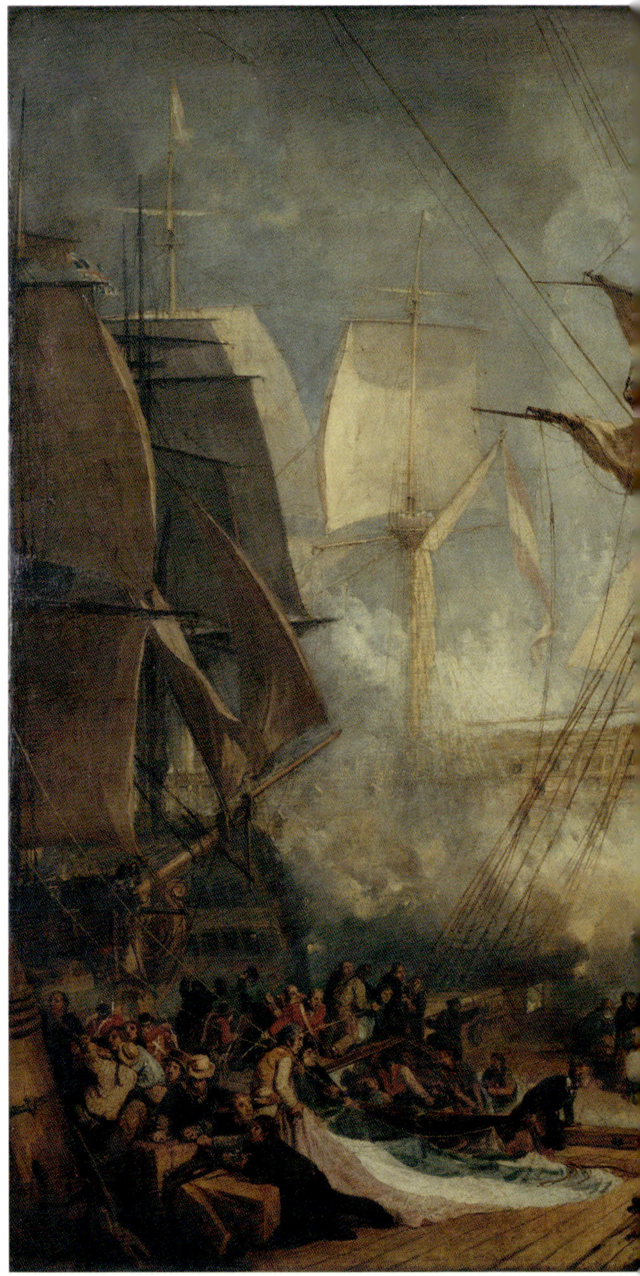

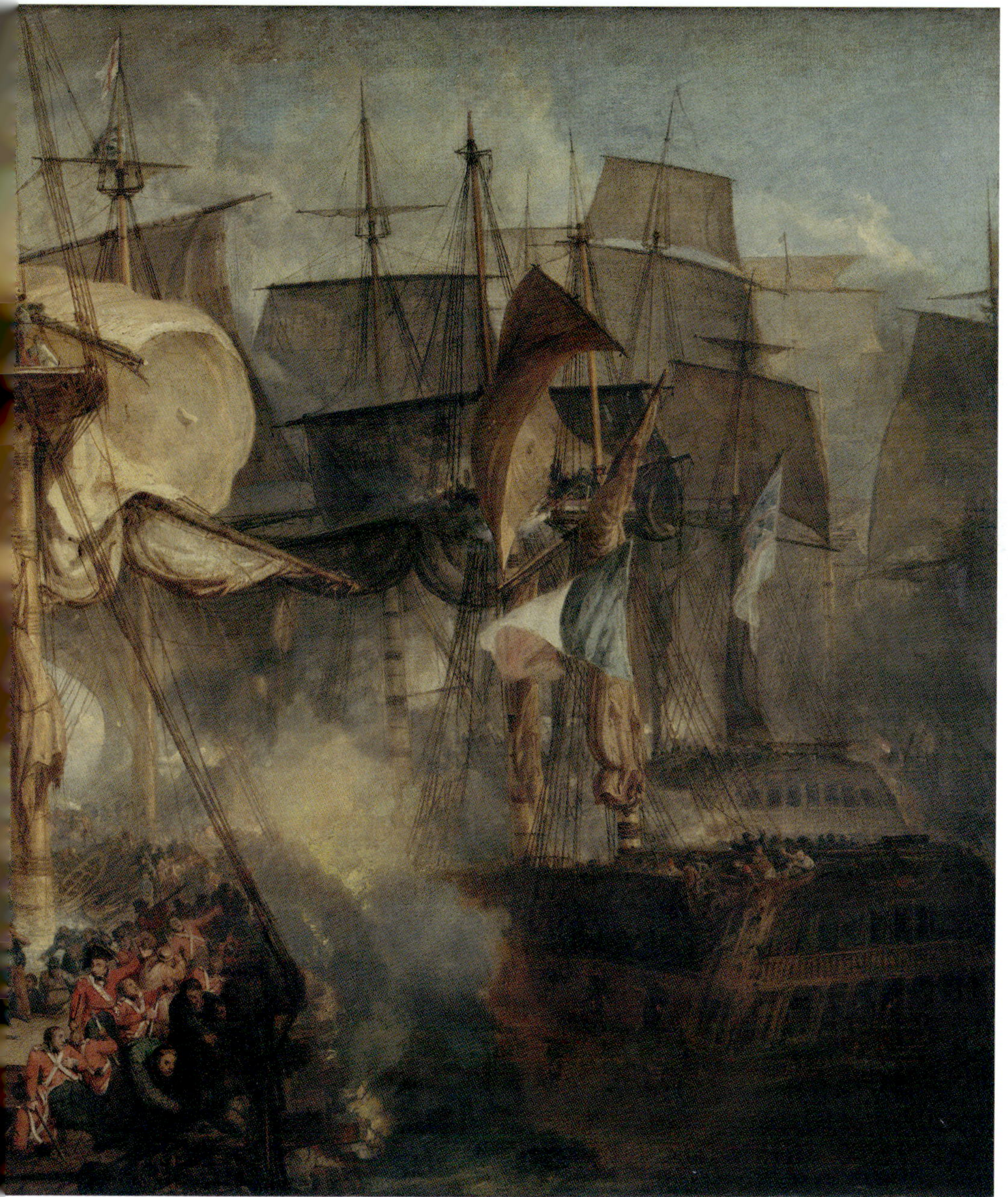

Chapter 2
The Painting

King George IV's love of spectacle and extravagance shaped his public reputation. Throughout his life, he lavished vast sums of money on art, architecture and fashion, becoming a pioneering cultural patron. Yet his profligate spending and decadent habits made him unpopular. Although his status as heir to the throne meant he had not been permitted to undertake active military or naval service, he nevertheless wanted to associate himself with the triumphs of the Revolutionary and Napoleonic Wars. At Windsor Castle, he created the 'Waterloo Chamber'. Taking its name from the final battle of the conflict, this chamber was lined with portraits of the monarchs, statesmen and generals who had led the alliance that defeated Napoleon on land. The war at sea, meanwhile, was the focus of the displays that the King installed at St James's Palace.

As Prince of Wales, George had acquired a vast painting of *The Battle of the Glorious First of June* by the artist Philippe Jacques de Loutherbourg (1740–1812, fig. 10). Named for the date on which it took place, this action was fought between British and French fleets in the North Atlantic in summer 1794. Although the outcome was disputed, the British regarded themselves as the victors. De Loutherbourg painted the subject for the print publishers Valentine Green and Christian von Mechel in 1795. After releasing an engraving of the painting for public sale, Green and Von Mechel sold the original to the Liverpool-based auctioneer Thomas Vernon, from whom it was purchased by the Prince of Wales in the early 1800s.

Two decades later, George, now king, decided to commission a corresponding image of the Battle of Trafalgar to hang alongside De Loutherbourg's painting at St James's Palace. Together, the pair would represent the first and last major sea battles of the recent wars against France, creating a grand celebration of British naval glory. Following a recommendation from the President of the Royal Academy, Sir Thomas Lawrence (1769–1830), the King hired Turner to produce the Trafalgar picture in 1822. Turner eventually received £500 for the work, but he had to ask repeatedly for the final instalment of his fee, which was not paid until June 1826 – two years after the painting's completion.

FIG. 10
The Battle of the Glorious First of June,
Philippe Jacques de Loutherbourg,
1795,
oil on canvas,
2,665 × 3,735mm,
BHC0470

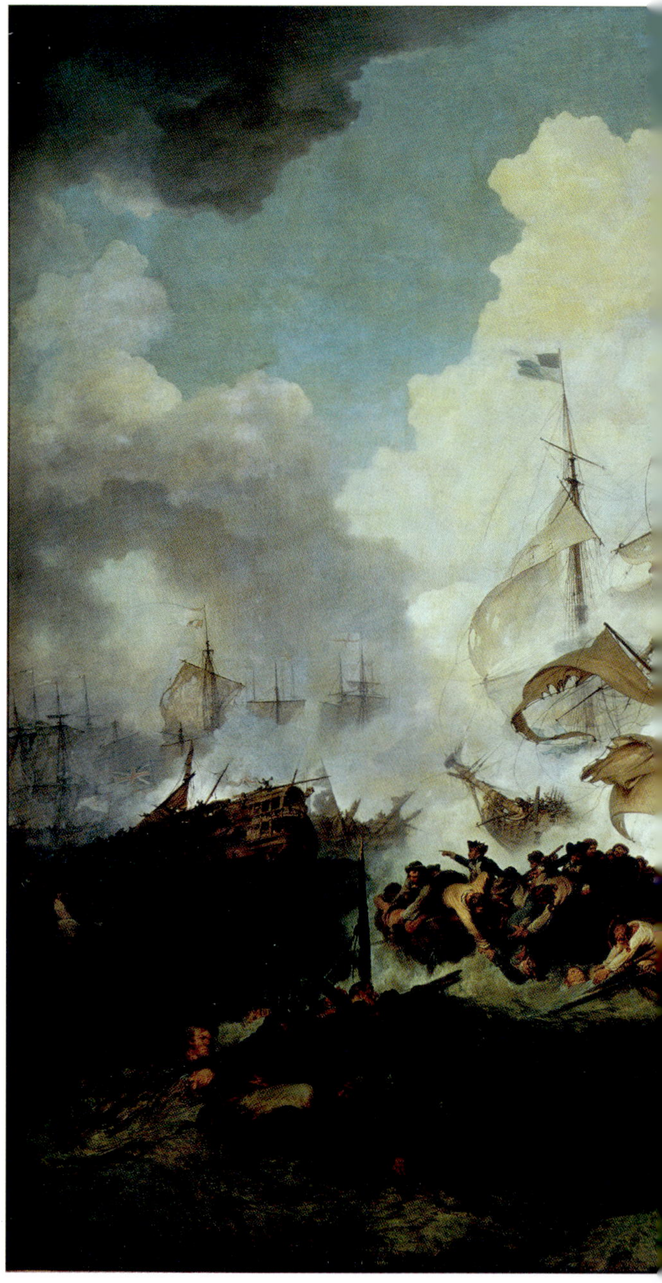

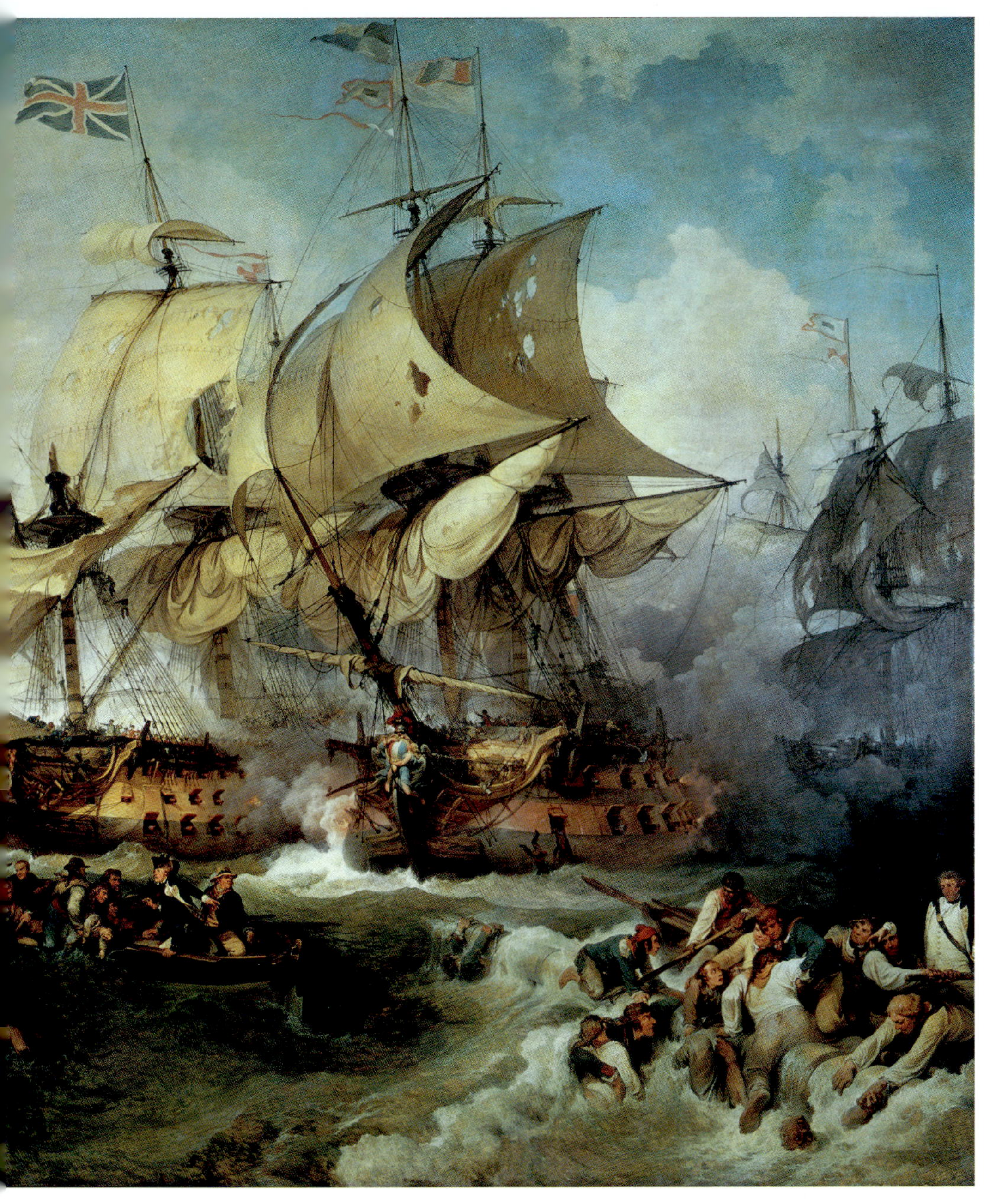

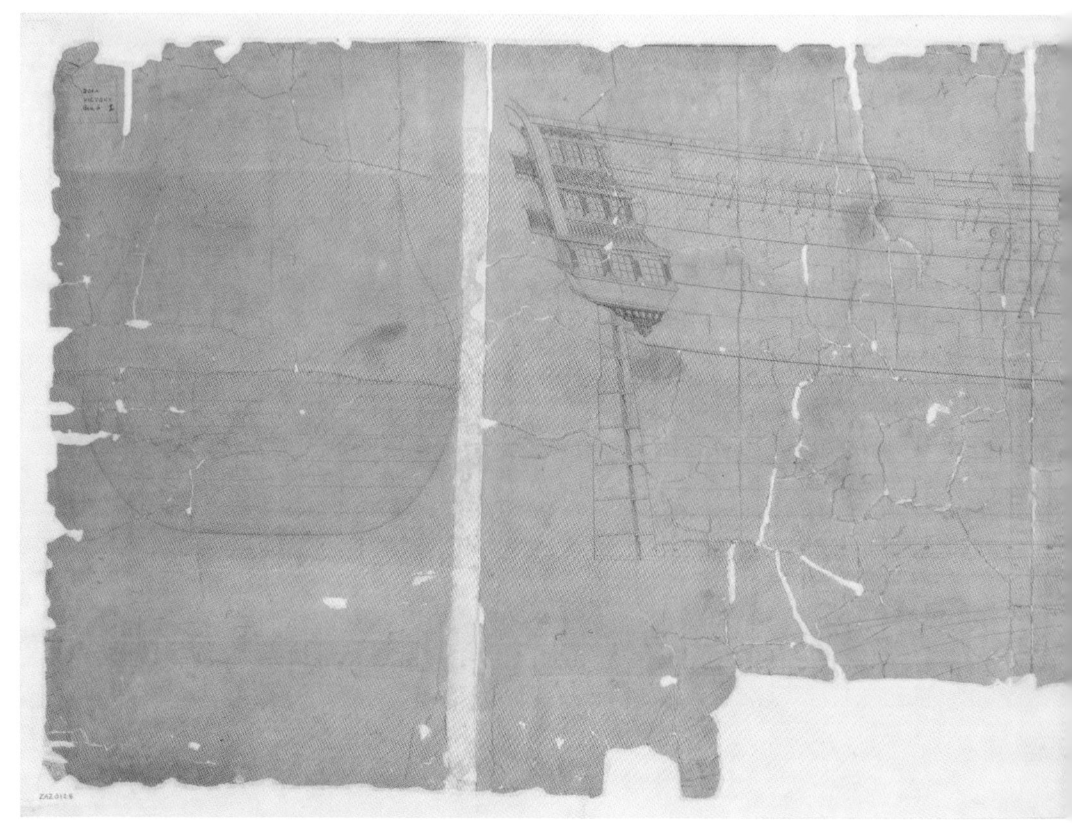

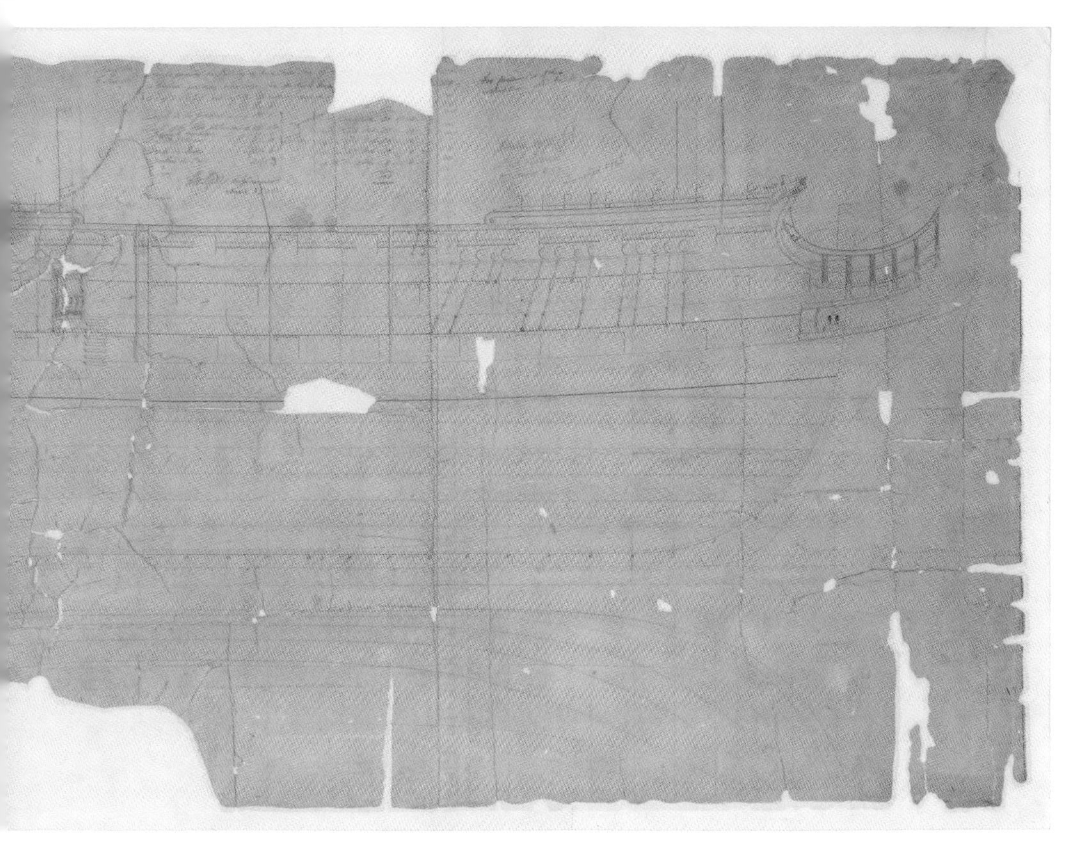

FIG. 11
'Victory' (1765),
Thomas Slade,
1759,
pen and ink on paper,
703 × 1,905mm,
ZAZ0128

Turner's earlier painting, *The Battle of Trafalgar, as Seen from the Mizen Starboard Shrouds of the 'Victory'*, had been completed in the years immediately following the battle. Now he faced the challenge of reimagining the action after more than a decade had elapsed. His new picture would be shaped by the political and cultural context of the 1820s, as well as by the specific requirements of the King's commission, including the need to respond to De Loutherbourg's painting.

Nelson and the *Victory*

As he set to work on the project, Turner was able to draw upon the studies of the *Victory* that he had made at Sheerness in late 1805. However, he also sought to gather additional materials. From the Admiralty, he borrowed a plan of the *Victory*'s hull (fig. 11), and, in December 1823, he solicited assistance from the marine painter John Christian Schetky (1778–1874), who taught drawing at the Royal Naval College in Portsmouth.

At Turner's request, Schetky made sketches of the *Victory* while it was undergoing repairs in Portsmouth Harbour. An idea of what these sketches were like can be gleaned from a slightly later drawing, dated 26 August 1824 (fig. 12). This sketch shows the starboard side of the *Victory*, although Schetky noted underneath that 'the ship canted [tilted] while this was being made – and is therefore much too long'. His annotation highlights the difficulty of making accurate drawings during the repair works. Turner himself recognised the limited usefulness of drawings that showed the vessel in its present state. Acknowledging that the *Victory* had 'undergone considerable alterations since the action', he reassured Schetky that 'a slight sketch' would suffice. Turner also asked Schetky if he had any drawings of other ships that had fought at Trafalgar, including the Spanish *Santísima Trinidad* and the French *Redoutable*, from which the shot that killed Nelson was fired.

Turner's correspondence with Schetky gives the impression that he was apprehensive about trying to recreate the appearance of a battle that had happened over a decade previously. This nervousness may also explain why he painted two preliminary studies, in which he experimented with different ideas for the composition (figs 13 and 14). In both sketches, the battle rages in the distance behind the towering form of the *Victory*, which occupies the centre of the image. The ship is seen from a distance across an expanse of sea. In the second sketch, this space is filled with boats and groups of figures, including sailors fighting for survival in the water. The final painting follows the general arrangement of this sketch, although Turner did make some amendments. These included altering the angle of the French ship on the right,

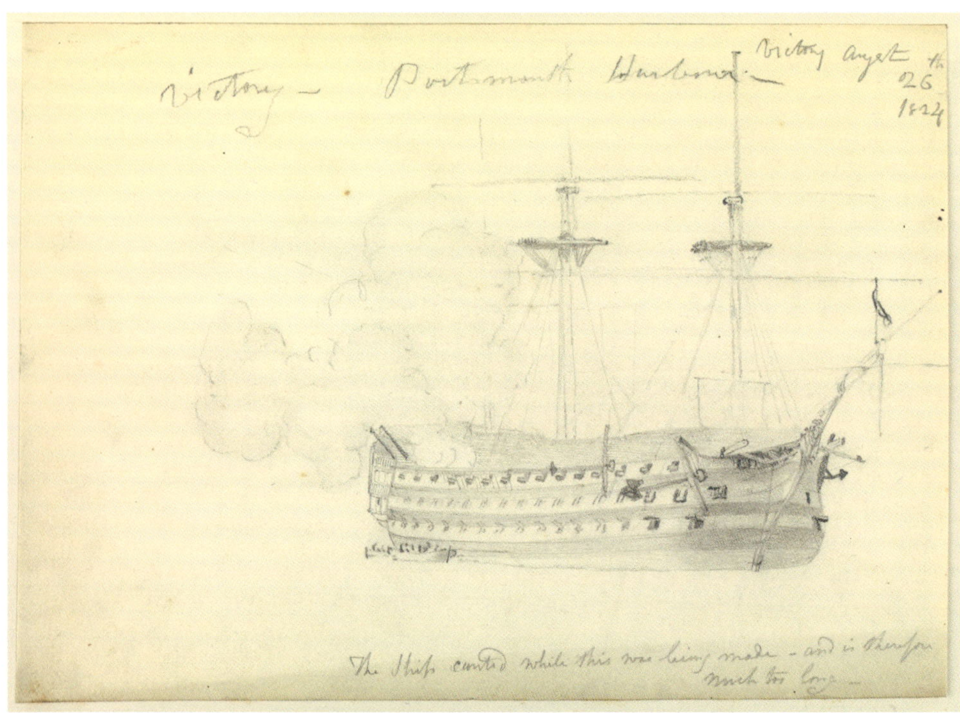

FIG. 12
'Victory' in
Portsmouth Harbour,
John Christian Schetky,
1824,
graphite on paper,
202 × 277mm,
PAI0907

changing the positions of the *Victory*'s sails and reconfiguring the groups in the foreground. De Loutherbourg's *Battle of the Glorious First of June* featured a similar combination of people in the sea and ships in the distance, suggesting that Turner modelled his composition on the earlier picture.

Born in the French city of Strasbourg, De Loutherbourg travelled widely, eventually settling in London, where he made his name designing costumes, sets and special effects for the Drury Lane Theatre in the 1770s. His most famous work was the Eidophusikon, a mechanical theatre that used mirrors and pulleys to create moving images, recreating sunsets, storms and erupting volcanoes. This theatrical experience shaped De Loutherbourg's subsequent career as a painter. His pictures frequently featured dramatic light effects and stage-like compositions. *The Battle of the Glorious First of June* is no exception. The focus of the image is the duel between the *Queen Charlotte* and the *Montagne*, the respective flagships of the British commander-in-chief, Admiral Richard Howe (1726–99), and his French counterpart, Rear-Admiral Louis-Thomas Villaret-Joyeuse (1747–1812). With smoke billowing from their guns, the two warships loom like hulking pieces of stage scenery behind the human drama playing out in the foreground, where British boats race to rescue drowning French sailors from the waves.

FIG. 13
First Sketch for 'The Battle of Trafalgar',
J.M.W. Turner,
about 1823,
oil on canvas,
902 × 1,213mm,
Tate

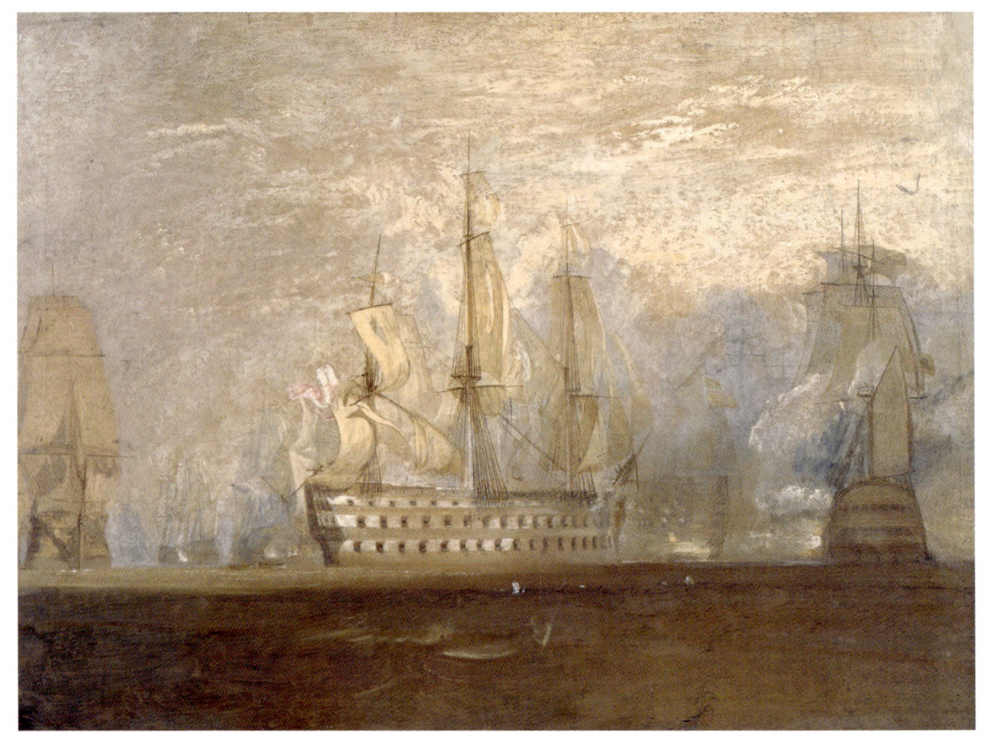

FIG. 14
Second Sketch for 'The Battle of Trafalgar',
J.M.W. Turner,
about 1823,
oil on canvas,
902 × 1,213mm,
Tate

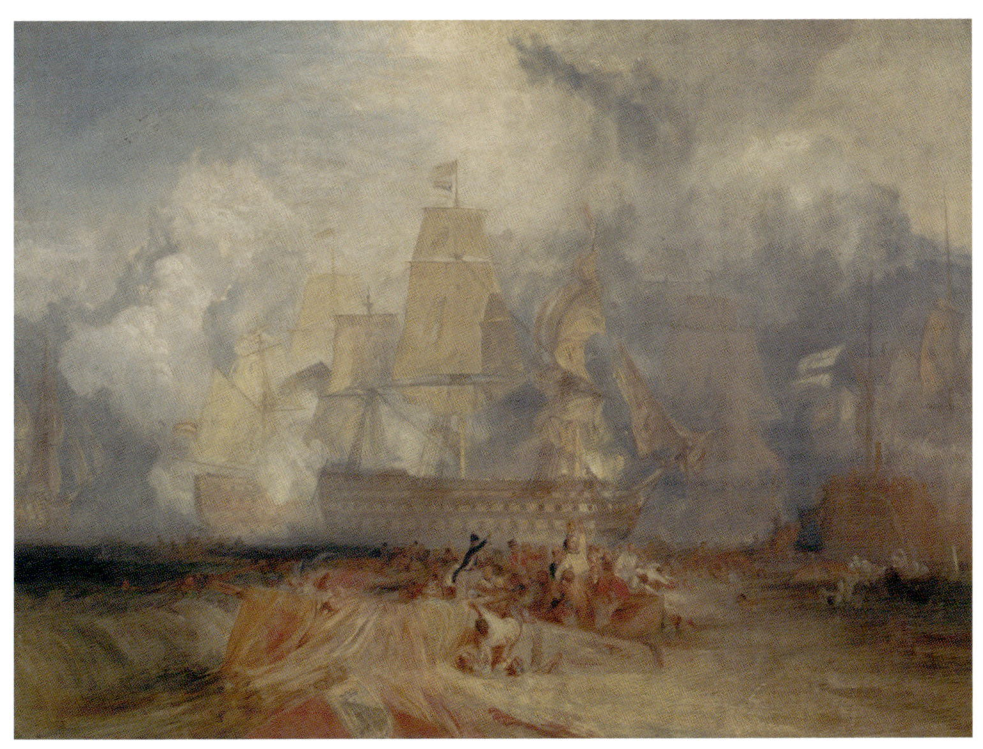

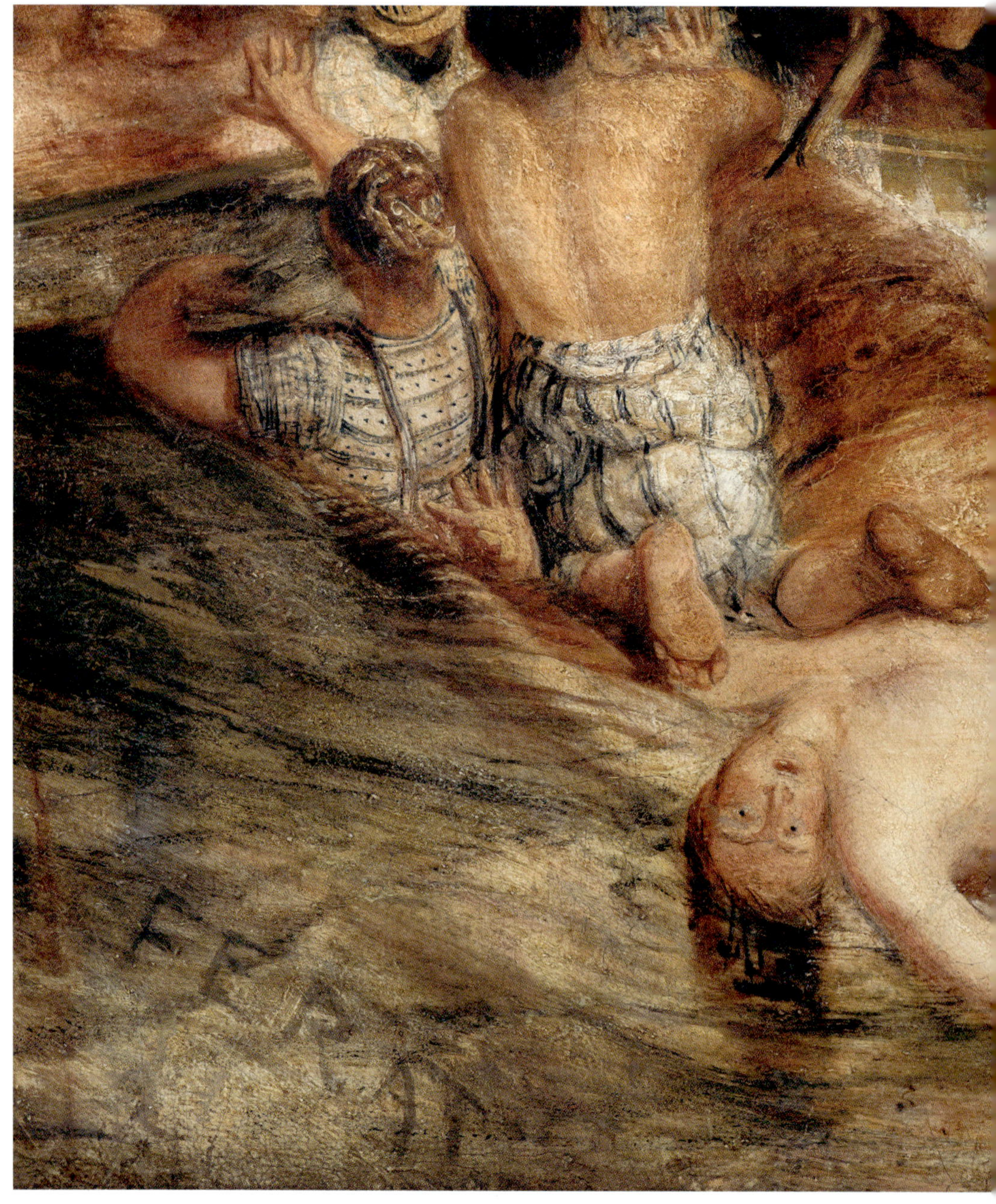

Turner admired De Loutherbourg's pictures and appreciated the opportunity to create a visual response to his work. Yet representing the Battle of Trafalgar posed a unique challenge, since the event was remembered as much for Nelson's death as it was for the clash between the two fleets. Turner had ingeniously solved this problem in his earlier painting, *The Battle of Trafalgar as Seen from the Mizen Starboard Shrouds of the 'Victory'*, through the adoption of an elevated viewpoint in the rigging of the flagship. This perspective afforded a view looking down on Nelson's collapse and another looking out across the wider battle. However, having decided to follow De Loutherbourg's example in placing the *Victory* in the distance, Turner could not make use of the same conceit again.

Unable to show Nelson's fatal wounding, Turner instead littered his painting with symbolic allusions to the Vice-Admiral's fate. The final word of Nelson's Latin motto, 'Palmam qui meruit ferat', has been scrawled across the waves in the foreground (fig. 15). This phrase literally meant: 'Let him who has earned it bear the palm.' Palm branches were a traditional symbol of victory, hence a looser translation would be: 'Victory comes to those who fight for it.'

Further phrases associated with Nelson are represented through the signal flags that fly from the *Victory*'s mainmast.

FIG. 15 Detail of *The Battle of Trafalgar*, Nelson's motto in the waves

In the moments before the battle, Nelson famously ordered Lieutenant John Pasco (1774–1853) to send the following signal to the fleet: 'England expects that every man will do his duty.' Nelson's wording originally featured the verb 'confides', meaning 'is confident', but Pasco recommended using 'expects' instead. The substitution enabled him to send the message faster, since there was a shorthand for 'expects' within the flag code for naval signals.

There was no shorthand for 'duty', however, so this word had to be spelt out one letter at a time. The flags in Turner's painting spell out the final three letters, 'U', 'T' and 'Y'. Each letter is represented with a pair of flags, and a final yellow-and-blue flag serves as punctuation, denoting the end of the message (fig. 16). In highlighting the word 'duty', Turner created a double reference, alluding not only to the 'England expects' signal from the start of the battle but also to Nelson's dying words, as they had been reported in the contemporary press: 'Thank God I have done my duty.'

A final acknowledgement of Nelson's death is provided through the *Victory*'s toppling foremast. This detail deviated from the facts of the battle. In reality, the ship had lost its mizzenmast (the rearmost mast). Turner, however, showed the foremast sustaining damage instead because this mast carried Nelson's command flag, a white-and-red Saint George's

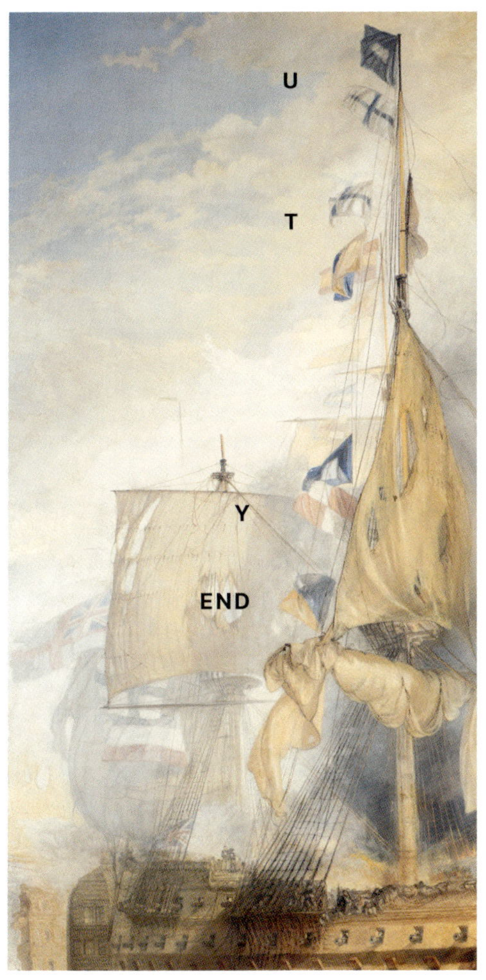

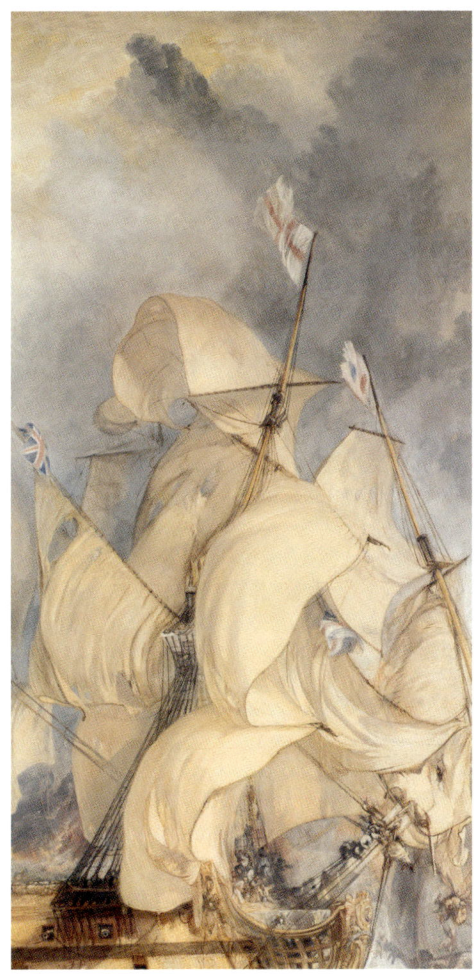

FIG. 16
Detail of *The Battle of Trafalgar* (annotated), signal flags from the *Victory*'s mainmast

FIG. 17
Detail of *The Battle of Trafalgar*, the *Victory*'s falling foremast

Cross (fig. 17). Admirals, vice-admirals and rear-admirals were entitled to fly the flag of their squadron – red, white or blue – from one of their ship's masts, giving rise to the term 'flagship' for a senior commander's vessel. Which mast carried the flag depended on the officer's rank: mizzen for a rear-admiral, fore for a vice-admiral and main for an admiral. At Trafalgar, Nelson was Vice-Admiral of the White, hence the *Victory* flew the Saint George's Cross (the flag of the white squadron) from its foremast. The fall of this mast in Turner's painting therefore served as a metaphor for the Vice-Admiral's demise.

Ships and sailors

As well as suggesting Nelson's fate, Turner also attempted to encapsulate the sprawling and chaotic contest between the two fleets. To the right of the *Victory*, the French ship *Redoutable* lists to one side, its bow sinking beneath the waves (fig. 18). This was another creative liberty on Turner's part: although the *Redoutable* had surrendered during the battle, it had not foundered until the following day. In compressing this timeline, Turner emphasised Britain's triumph. The sinking vessel acts as a symbol of the allied fleet's defeat.

More ships surround the *Victory* and the *Redoutable*, but it is difficult to see them through the clouds of smoke.

FIG. 18 Detail of *The Battle of Trafalgar*, the sinking *Redoutable*

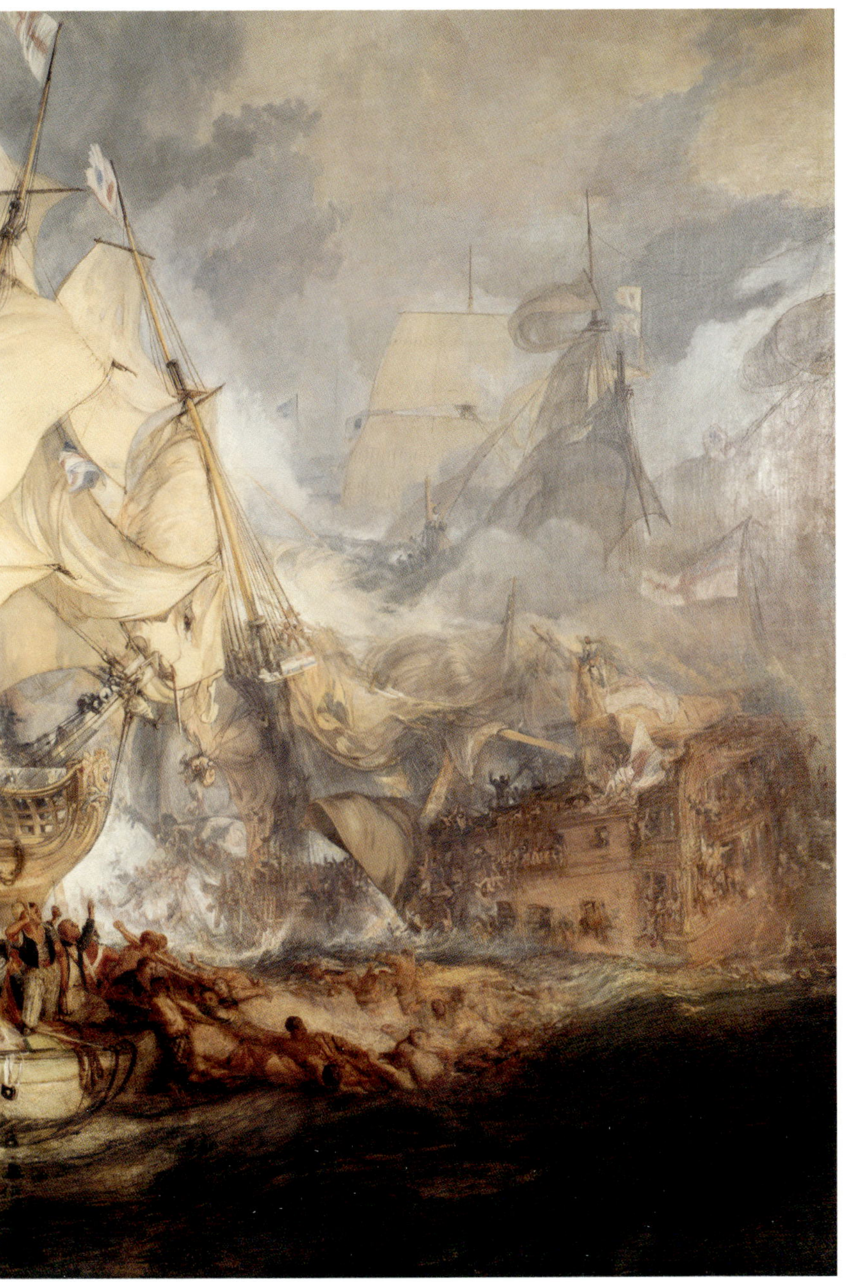

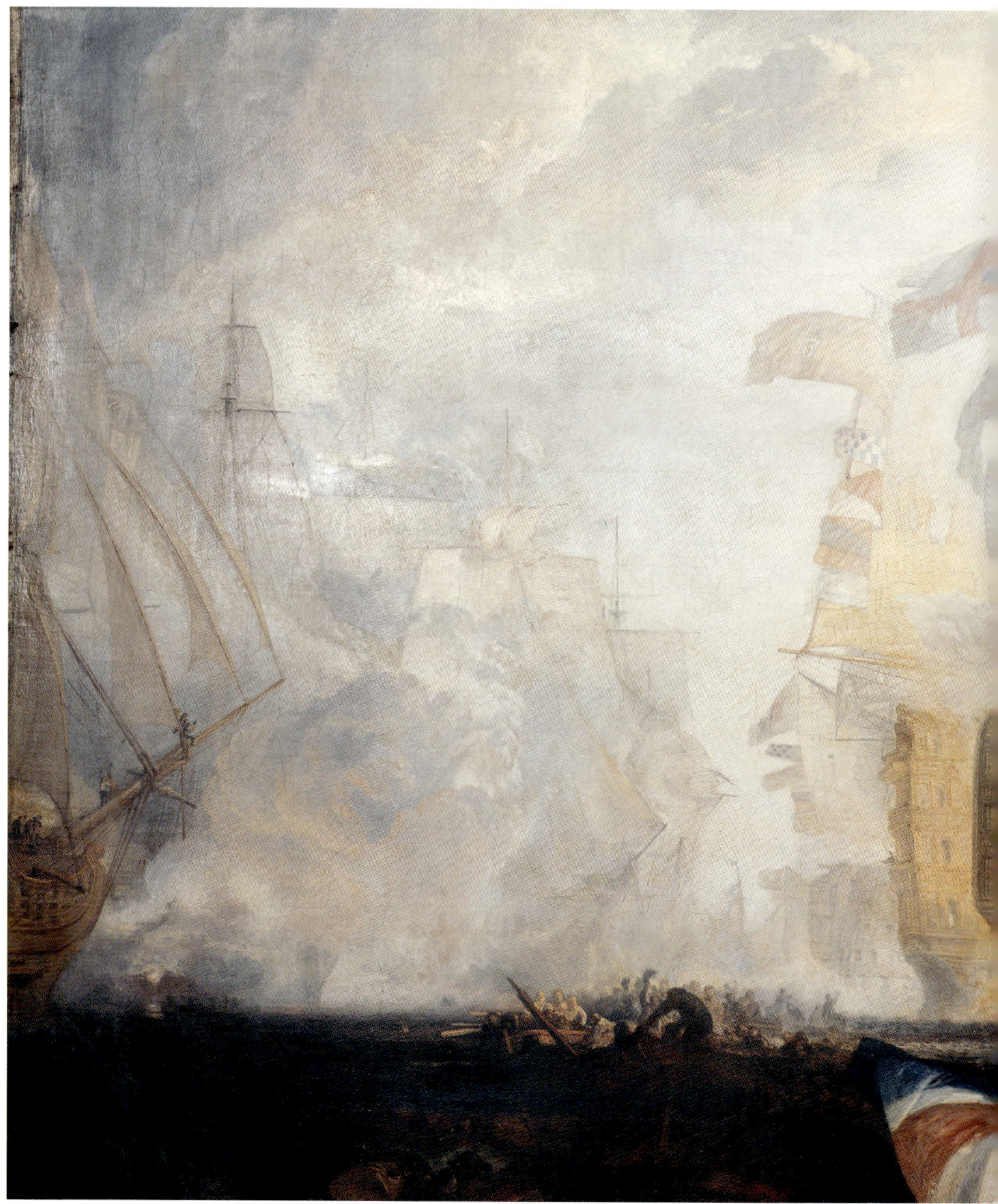

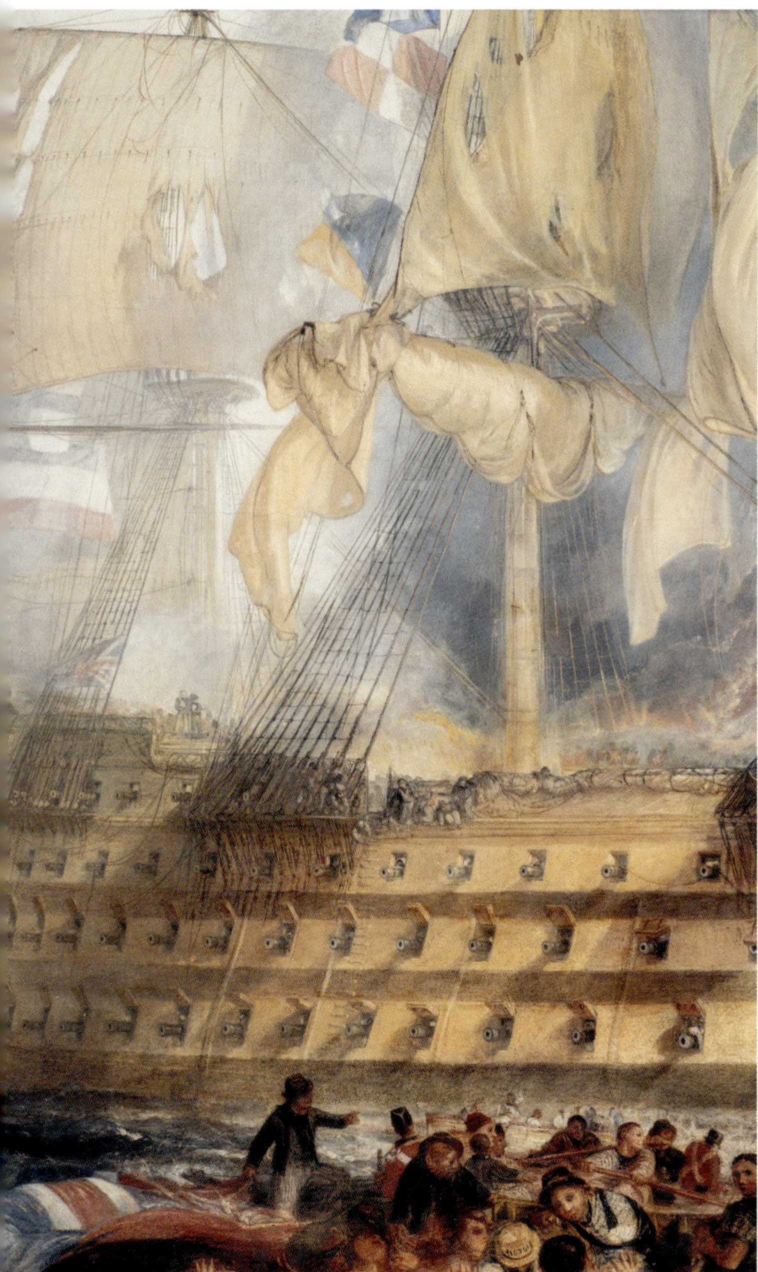

FIG. 19
Detail of *The Battle of Trafalgar*, the *Neptune* entering from the left in front of the burning *Achille*, with the illuminated stern of the *Santísima Trinidad* behind the *Victory* and the *Bucentaure* beyond

Some individual vessels are identifiable, including the British ship *Neptune*, which enters the picture on the far left beside the French *Achille* (fig. 19). The latter is engulfed in flames. Further fires illuminate the stern of the Spanish flagship *Santísima Trinidad*, which is immediately behind the *Victory*. Beyond that is the *Bucentaure*, the flagship of Vice-Admiral Pierre-Charles Villeneuve (1763–1806), the commander-in-chief of the combined fleet. However, the overall impression is one of confusion. Overlapping hulls, sails and masts stretch back to the horizon, evoking the brutal close-range fighting that ensued after Nelson ordered his ships to break the allied line.

Importantly, Turner does not hide the human cost of this violence. The painting is crammed with people, from the decks and rigging of the ships to the small boats and churning waves in the foreground. Many of these individuals face danger and death. Several sailors tumble into the water from the *Redoutable*, while their crewmates cling desperately to the sinking ship's ropes (fig. 20). In the sea, drowning men scramble over one another in search of safety. The groups in the boats extend their arms and oars towards those in distress, but some are already submerged with only a hand or foot remaining above the surface. This horrifying life-and-death struggle fills the foreground of the painting, compelling the viewer to bear witness to it. The focal point is a shirtless sailor, lying across a tangle of spars and rigging, close to where Nelson's motto is inscribed (fig. 21). The sailor's suffering subverts the noble ideals of victory and sacrifice evoked in the motto. His head lolls to one side, staring out at the viewer as the waves threaten to overwhelm him.

Within the artistic tradition of marine painting, it was unusual to devote so much attention to the plight of seafarers. Marine paintings tended to show battles from a distance, focusing on the positions and movements of ships, rather than the actions of their crews. Human figures are often no more than specks, if they are visible at all. This approach is exemplified in Nicholas Pocock's treatment of the Battle of Trafalgar in a pair of paintings from around 1808 (figs 22 and 23). These pictures were made to be reproduced as illustrations in James Stanier Clarke and John McArthur's two-volume biography of Nelson, published in 1809. One painting represented the start of the battle, the other its conclusion. Both adopt a bird's eye view, looking down on the ships from a distance. This highlights the intersecting lines of the two fleets at the commencement of the action and the subsequent fragmentation of the fighting into a series of ship-to-ship skirmishes. The paintings function almost like diagrams, dispassionately and analytically mapping out the tactical phases of the battle. In Clarke and McArthur's publication, this didactic emphasis was reinforced through

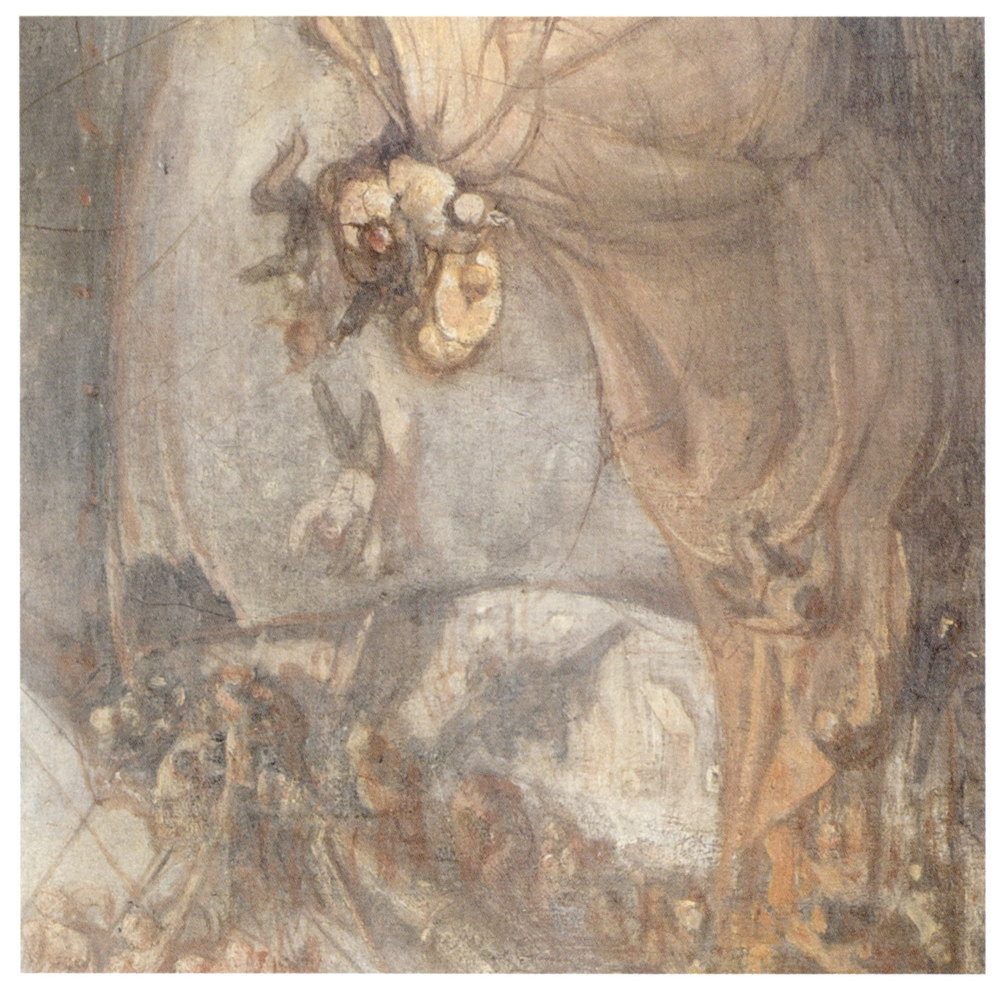

FIG. 20
Detail of *The Battle of Trafalgar*, a sailor falls from the *Redoutable*, while others cling to the ship's ropes

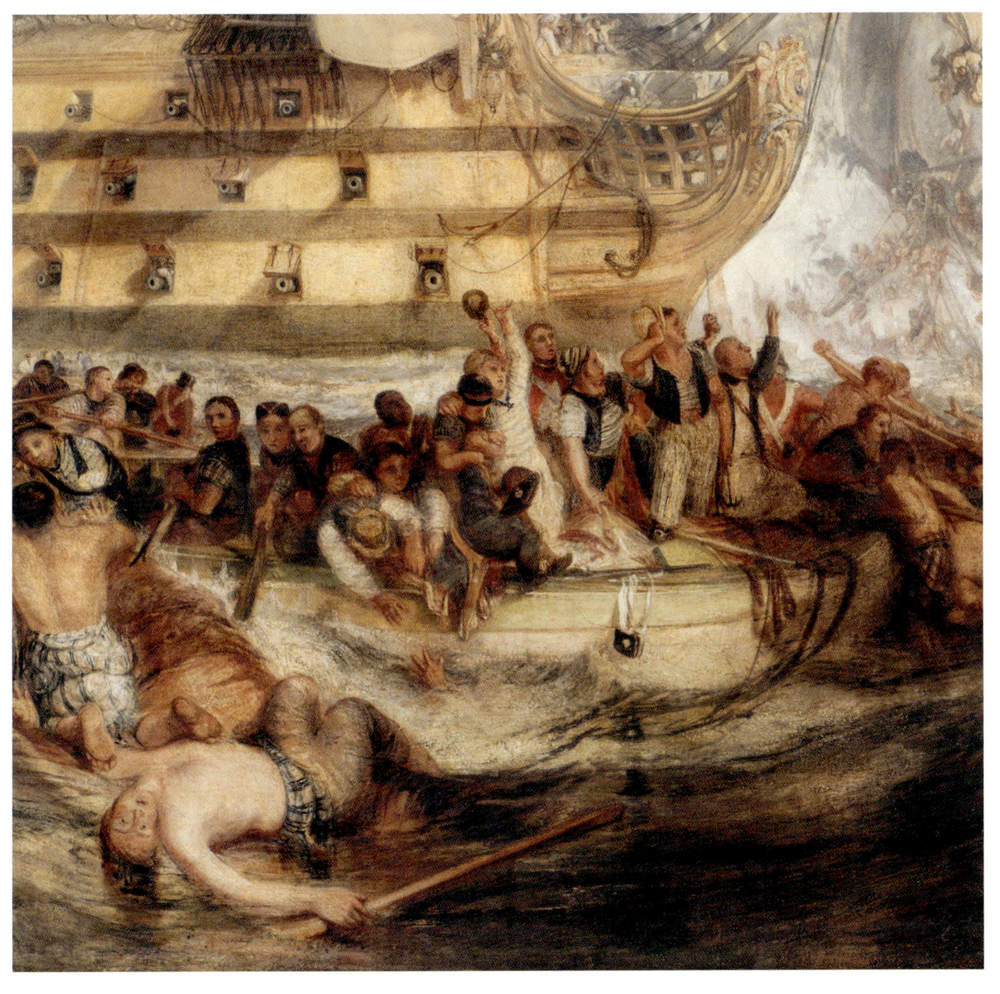

FIG. 21
Detail of *The Battle of Trafalgar*, a sailor caught in spars and rigging, while others scramble to find safety in small boats. In one of the boats, the sailors cheer the destruction of the *Redoutable*

FIG. 22
The Battle of Trafalgar,
21 October 1805:
Beginning of the Action,
Nicholas Pocock,
about 1808,
oil on canvas,
712 × 1,016mm,
BHC0548

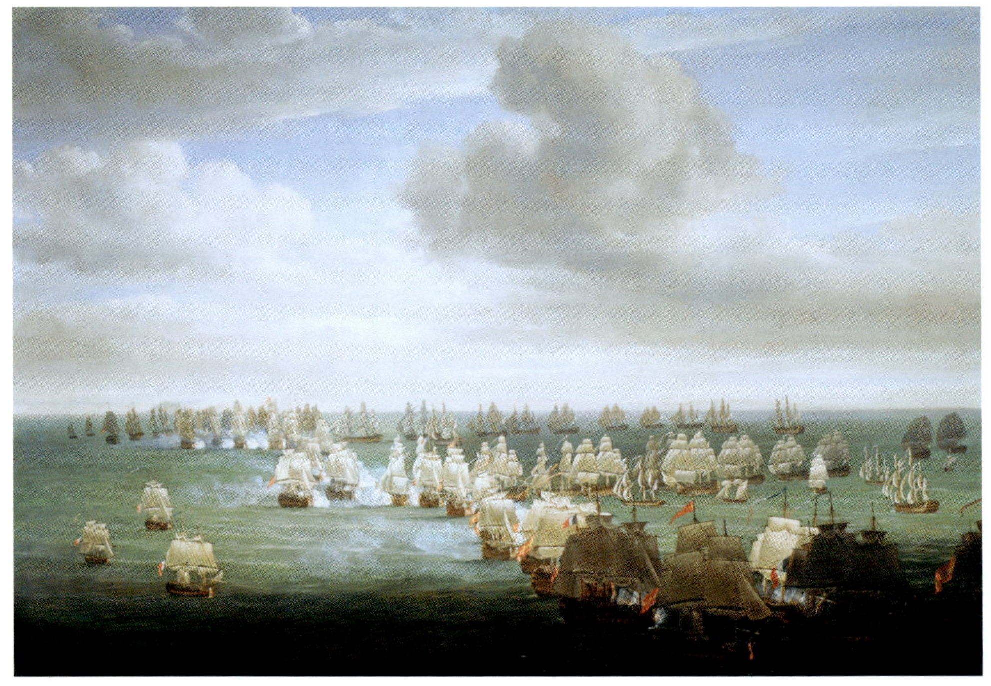

FIG. 23
The Battle of Trafalgar, 21 October 1805: End of the Action, Nicholas Pocock, about 1808, oil on canvas, 711 × 1,016mm, BHC0549

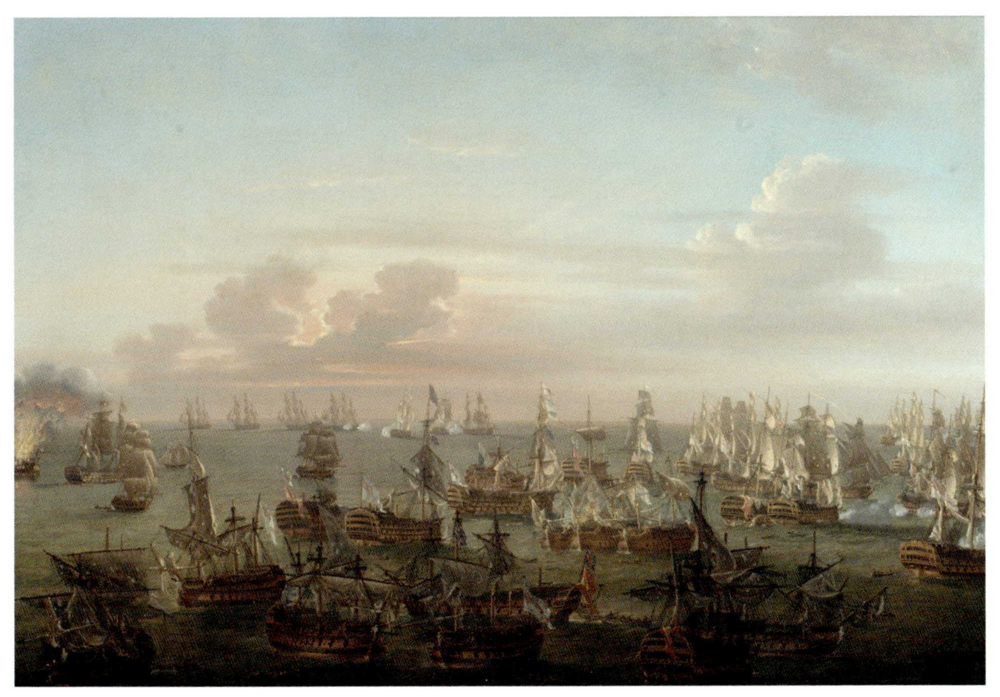

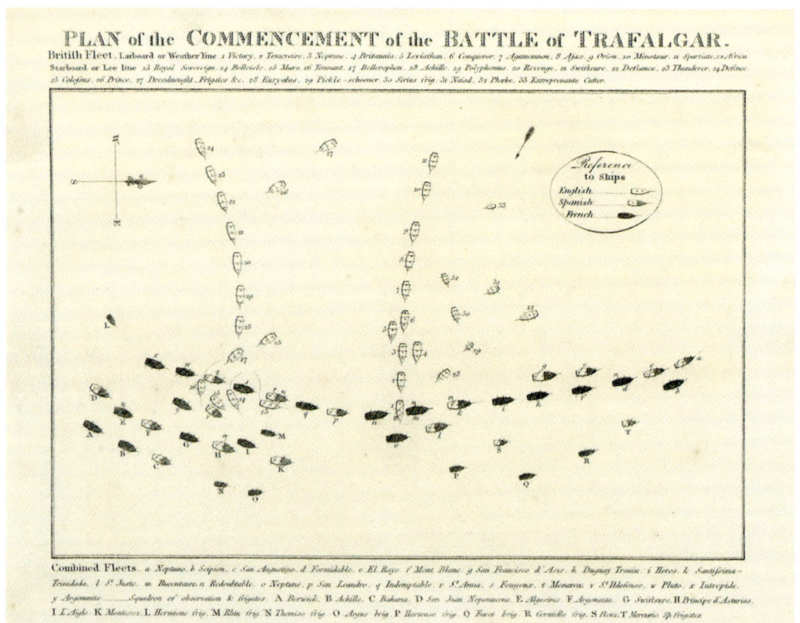

the printing of battle plans alongside the two images (figs 24 and 25).

Turner's approach could not be more different. He eschewed factual accuracy in favour of evoking the visceral experience of Trafalgar for those who fought. In this respect, the painting echoed his earlier exploration of the horrors of war in *The Field of Waterloo* (fig. 26), which commemorated the

FIG. 24 *Plan of the Commencement of the Battle of Trafalgar*, after Nicholas Pocock, 1809, engraving on paper, 280 × 330mm, PAD4051

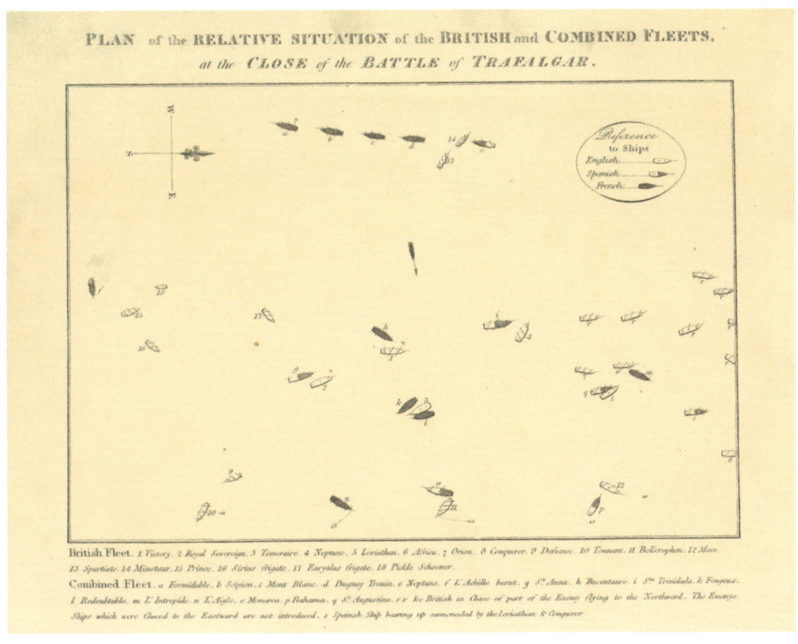

final defeat of Napoleon's army in June 1815. Turner visited the battlefield in August 1817 and completed his painting the following year. Rather than celebrating his nation's victory, he highlighted the bloody aftermath of the battle. Dead and wounded soldiers from both sides lie heaped in the foreground. A rocket explodes in the night sky, illuminating the field for the survivors, friends and family members who are searching

FIG. 25 *Plan of the Relative Situation of the British and Combined Fleets, at the Close of the Battle of Trafalgar*, after Nicholas Pocock, 1809, engraving on paper, 277 × 330mm, PAD5716

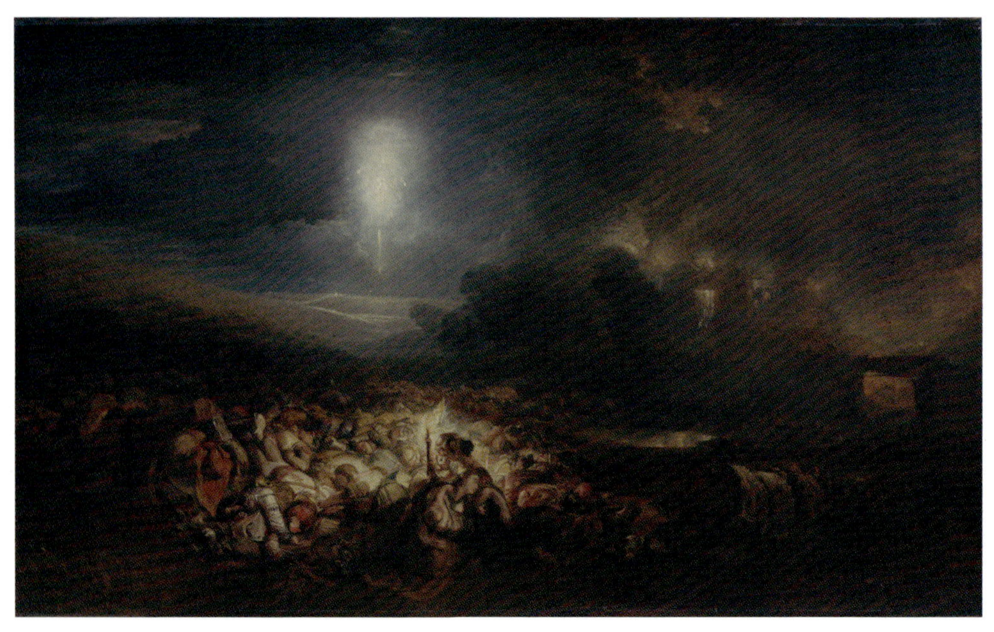

FIG. 26
The Field of Waterloo,
J.M.W. Turner,
1818,
oil on canvas,
1,473 × 2,388mm,
Tate

for their comrades and loved ones among the fallen. There is no sense of glory, only loss.

The Battle of Trafalgar is not as bleak as *The Field of Waterloo*. Even while lamenting the destruction wrought by war, the painting highlights Britain's triumph. Several British sailors in the foreground pause to cheer in celebration of the *Redoutable*'s fate, in spite of the horror that surrounds them. This may reflect the requirements of the commission. Since *The Field of Waterloo* was not painted for any particular patron, Turner had more freedom to offer an ambivalent portrayal of war. *The Battle of Trafalgar*, by contrast, was painted for King George IV. Destined for a royal palace, it was expected to promote Britain's naval might.

Yet Turner still draws attention to the labour and sacrifices of working-class sailors. In the 1820s, class tensions were running high in Britain. The post-war period witnessed an economic crisis, mass unemployment, poor harvests and new tariffs on grain. Many ordinary people faced poverty and hardship but had little voice at a time when only property owners could vote. Protests for political reform gathered momentum, even though the authorities responded with censorship and violent suppression. On one level, Turner's painting glossed over this fraught situation, offering a comforting and harmonious vision of loyal sailors dutifully serving under Nelson's leadership, without any hint of discontent. At the same time, the prominence of these sailors within the picture implies that working-class labour could no longer be taken for granted and was worthy of recognition.

Turner's sympathy towards the sailors is evident through the care that he has exercised in the depiction of their clothing. In the early nineteenth century, the Royal Navy only issued uniform for officers. Ordinary sailors wore 'slops' – ready-made working clothes available for purchase from the ship's purser, including canvas jackets, waistcoats and loose-fitting trousers. The latter were often made from blue-and-white striped fabric, as seen in *The Battle of Trafalgar*. Many of the men in the water, including the shirtless figure in the foreground, are dressed in striped legwear. The painting also reflects the variety of headgear that sailors wore, from knitted caps to straw boaters. One of the straw hats is inscribed 'Victory'. As well as referencing the outcome of the battle, this detail reflects the fashion among sailors to decorate their hat bands with the name of the ship in which they served.

Turner has also included two Black sailors, one in the boat in the foreground, his hands clasped as if praying, and the other swimming for safety (figs 27 and 28). The Royal Navy's need for manpower during wartime meant that it became a driver of global mobility, recruiting men from around the world,

FIG. 27 Detail of *The Battle of Trafalgar*, a group of sailors, including a Black sailor with clasped hands

FIG. 28 Detail of *The Battle of Trafalgar*, a Black sailor swimming for safety

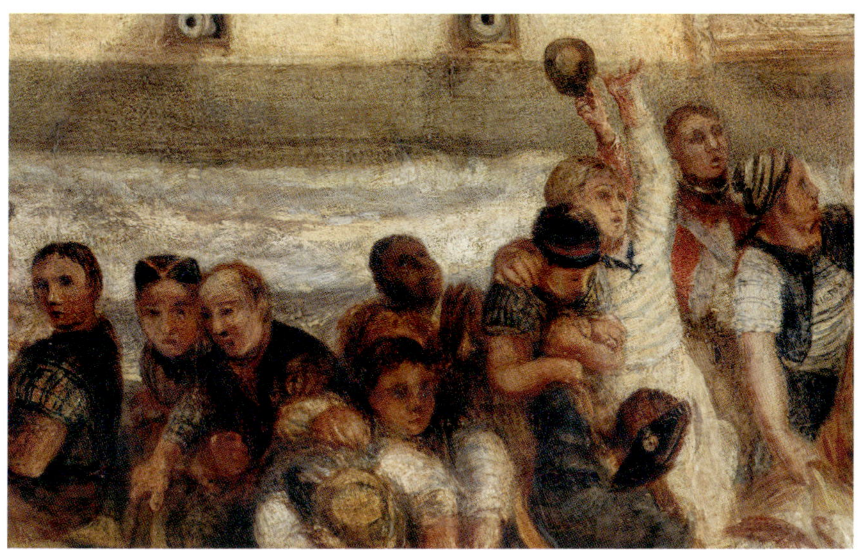

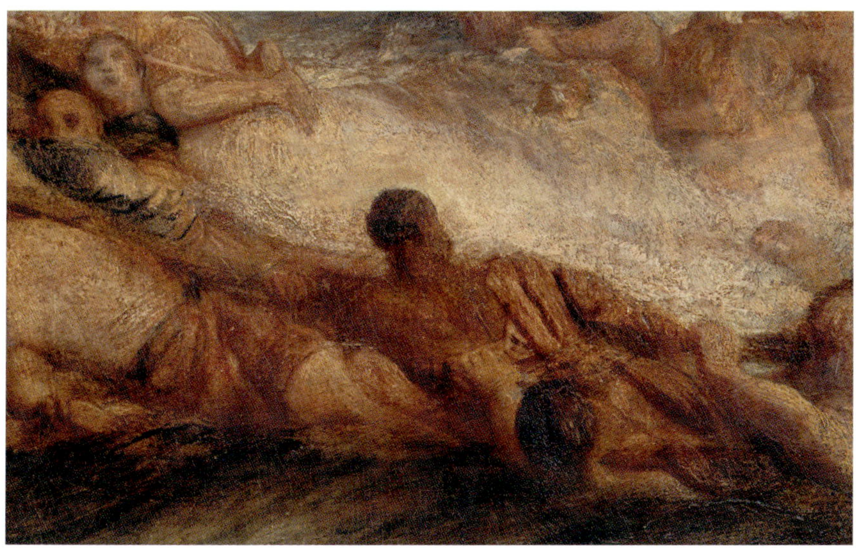

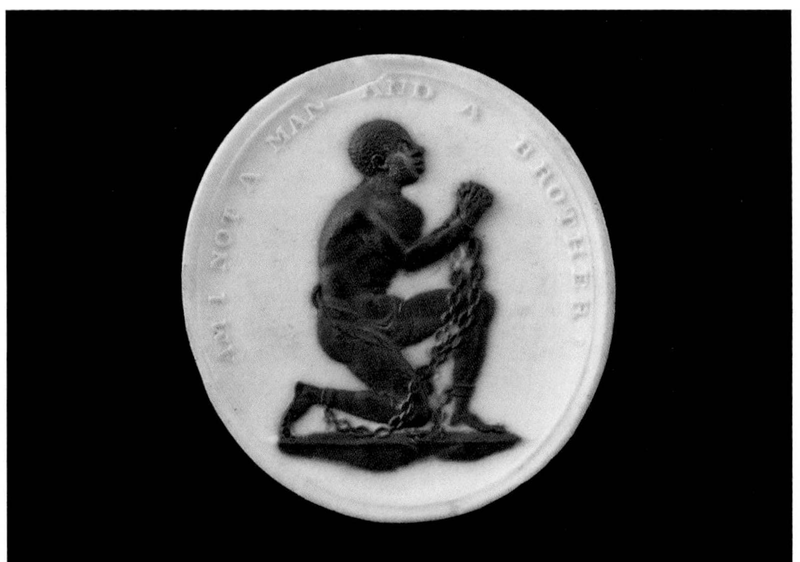

regardless of ethnicity, religion or nationality. Muster books from the time record the place of birth of every man who was present at the Battle of Trafalgar. As well as individuals from across the British Isles, these records include 18 men born in Africa and another 123 from the Caribbean. There were also sailors from Italy, Malta, India and the Americas. Turner's Black sailors are a reminder of this diversity.

With an upturned gaze and clasped hands, the pose of the Black sailor in the boat is reminiscent of Josiah Wedgwood's

FIG. 29 *London Abolition Committee medallion*, William Hackwood for Josiah Wedgwood, about 1787–90, glass, 30 × 27mm, ZBA2492

anti-slavery medallion (fig. 29). Designed as a seal for the Society for the Abolition of the Slave Trade in 1787, the medallion depicted a kneeling Black man with his manacled hands raised beneath the phrase, 'Am I not a man and a brother?' The image was widely reproduced, becoming one of the most recognisable symbols of the abolitionist movement in the years leading up to the passage of the Slave Trade Act of 1807, which outlawed the sale – but not the ownership – of enslaved people within the British Empire. The medallion exemplifies both the ideals and prejudices that underpinned the abolitionist movement. On the one hand, the design evoked a sense of shared humanity and charitable concern. At the same time, its Black African subject was presented as a helpless victim, pleading for British men and women to come to his rescue. This reinforced, or at least failed to challenge, the assumption of white supremacy that underpinned the Transatlantic Trade in Enslaved Africans.

Wedgwood's design began to circulate again in the 1820s as part of a renewed campaign to abolish enslavement, which culminated in the Slavery Abolition Act of 1833. This resurgence of abolitionism occurred while Turner was working on *The Battle of Trafalgar*. Although he had invested in a Jamaican cattle farm that used enslaved labour in 1805, Turner's liberal beliefs and his interest in current events meant that he was exposed to the campaigns and publications of the anti-slavery societies of his time. His most famous artistic engagement with the abolitionist cause came in 1840, when he exhibited *The Slave Ship* at the Royal Academy (fig. 30). This painting referenced an incident from 1781, in which more than 130 enslaved African people were murdered at sea.

Most art historians argue that Turner had been interested in abolitionism for at least a decade before he painted *The Slave Ship*, noting that he dedicated a print to the abolitionist politician John Joshua Proby, 1st Earl of Carysfort, in 1828. Often overlooked, the Black sailors in *The Battle of Trafalgar* may be evidence that Turner's engagement with the imagery and ideas of the anti-slavery movement began at least four years before the print dedication. In any case, these figures underscore the importance of seeing the painting in a global context, encompassing the intertwined histories of the Royal Navy, British colonialism, enslavement and abolition.

There are many layers of meaning within *The Battle of Trafalgar*. Turner endeavoured to transcend the facts of the battle, creating instead a deeply symbolic artwork that paid tribute to Nelson, dramatised Britain's victory, exposed the brutality of war and acknowledged the efforts of the sailors who manned the fleet. Yet, when the painting was unveiled in 1824, many viewers did not appreciate its complexity.

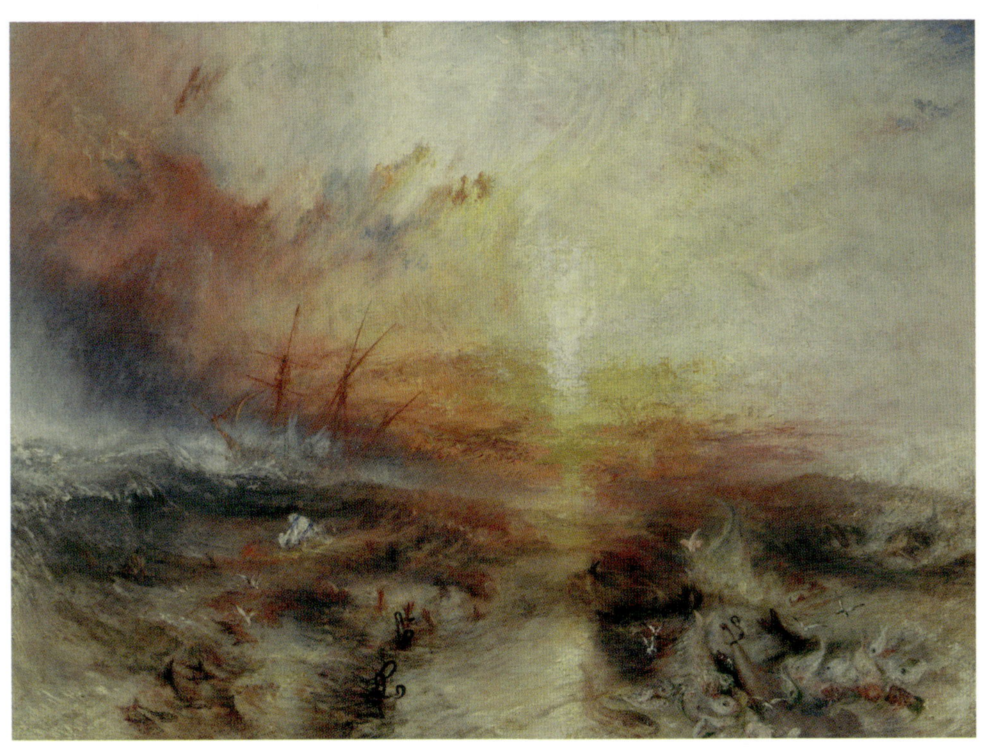

FIG. 30
The Slave Ship (Slavers Throwing Overboard the Dead and Dying, Typhoon Coming On), J.M.W. Turner, 1840, oil on canvas, 908 × 1,226mm, Museum of Fine Arts, Boston

Chapter 3

From St James's to Greenwich

On 27 May 1824, the artist Benjamin Robert Haydon (1786–1846) recorded in his diary that the government was 'not satisfied' with Turner's *The Battle of Trafalgar*. The painting had recently been installed at St James's Palace, hanging in the Ante Room alongside De Loutherbourg's *Battle of the Glorious First of June*. The two naval pictures flanked a portrait of the late King George III (fig. 31). This arrangement was mirrored in the adjoining Throne Room, where a portrait of the reigning monarch, George IV, was sandwiched between George Jones's paintings of the battlefields of Vitoria and Waterloo. Together, these displays celebrated war, victory and royal dynasty, linking naval triumphs from George III's reign with military campaigns fought during his son's regency.

As Benjamin Robert Haydon's comments indicate, *The Battle of Trafalgar* met with an unfavourable response. After receiving negative feedback from courtiers, government ministers and naval commanders, Turner spent 11 days making amendments to the painting in situ. Walter Thornbury, Turner's biographer, recorded that the artist 'altered the rigging to suit the fancy of every fresh critic', but his efforts failed to quiet the complaints. Even the King's brother, the Duke of Clarence (later William IV (reigned 1830–37)), expressed an opinion. The Duke, who was himself a naval officer, reportedly had an acrimonious exchange with Turner, telling the artist, 'I have been at sea the greater part of my life, Sir, you don't know who you are talking to, and I'll be damned if you know what you are talking about.'

Ultimately, the painting was only displayed at St James's Palace for five years. In 1829, George IV ordered that it should be removed from the royal collection and donated to the National Gallery of Naval Art at Greenwich. Art historian Gerald Finley has described this relocation as a 'final humiliation' for the much-maligned picture. However, several critics praised the appropriateness of the painting's new home and even defended the work itself.

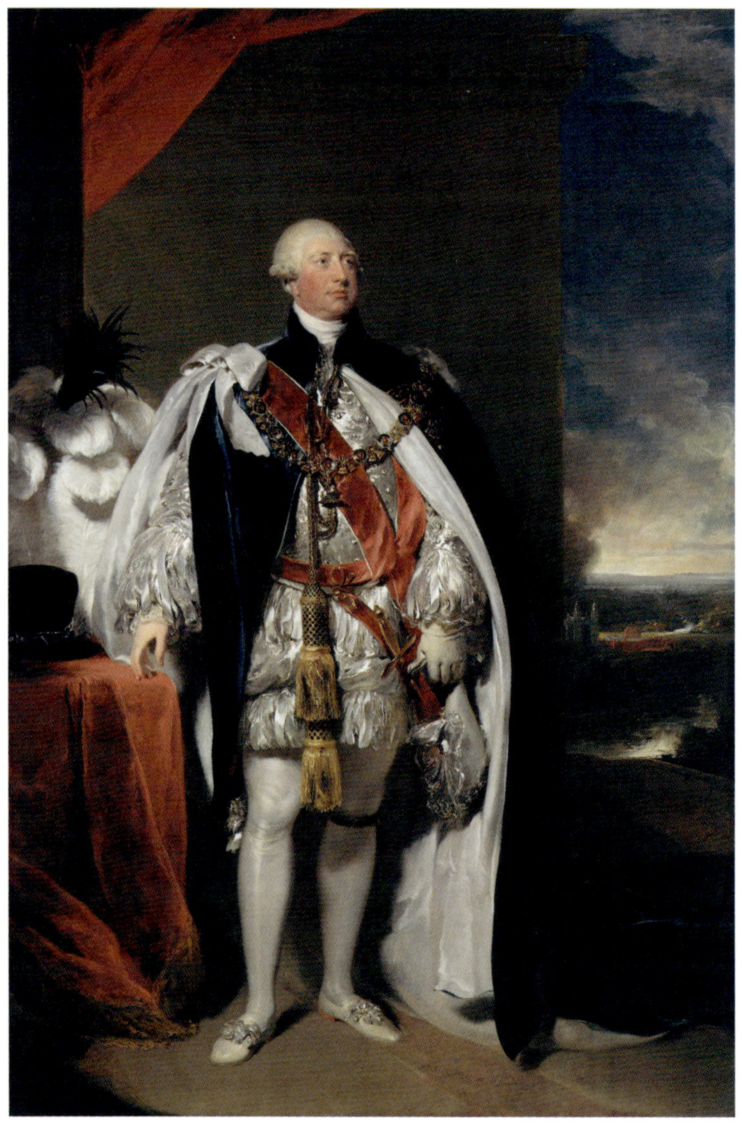

The critical response

The historian William James (1780–1827) was responsible for one of the most scathing critiques of the painting. His comments were published in the 1826 edition of his *Naval History of Great Britain* and in the *Literary Gazette*, a popular weekly magazine. James attacked the painting's 'glaring falsehoods and palpable inconsistencies', pointing out that it conflates several distinct phases of the battle:

> The telegraphic message ['England expects that every man will do his duty'] is going up, which was hoisted at about 11.40 a.m., the mizentopmast is falling, which went about 1 p.m., a strong light is reflected upon the *Victory*'s bow and sides from the burning *Achille*, which ship did not catch fire until 4.30 p.m., nor explode until 5.45 p.m. [...] and the *Redoutable* is sinking under the bows of the *Victory*, although the French ship did not sink until the night of the 22nd [October, the day after the battle], and then under the stern of the *Swiftsure*.

In James's view, these anachronisms meant it was impossible 'to say what time of the day, or what particular incident in the *Victory*'s proceedings' was being represented. He also

FIG. 31 *George III*, Thomas Lawrence, 1818–23, oil on canvas, 2,698 × 1,778mm, Royal Collection Trust

castigated Turner for inventing details, including the fall of the *Victory*'s foremast, which in reality 'never fell at all'.

Turner's intention had been to capture the human drama of the battle rather than the facts of the action, hence his willingness to take artistic liberties. James, however, insisted that a desire for 'pictorial effect' should never preclude an 'adherence to truth'. It was, he asserted, 'almost a national disgrace' that Britain lacked a single painting 'which, in accuracy of representation [...] is calculated to illustrate, and to stand as a lasting memorial of one of the greatest sea-battles that ever has been, or that perhaps ever will be fought'.

Other criticisms of the painting came from naval officers and sailors. According to art critic Dutton Cook (1829–83), Vice-Admiral Sir Thomas Masterman Hardy (1769–1839) – who had been Nelson's flag captain on the *Victory* – likened the painting to 'a street scene' and insisted that 'the ships had more the effect of houses than men-of-war'. Cook also recorded the views of an unnamed sailor, who described the picture as looking 'a damned deal more like a brickfield' than a naval battle. Brickfields were industrial sites, where clay was extracted from the ground, mixed with chalk and ash, moulded into bricks and fired in a kiln. Both Hardy and the sailor intended to disparage the lack of accurate nautical detail in the picture. Yet Turner may not have minded their analogies. Hardy's remark captures the hustle and bustle of the painting, which is crammed with people, not unlike a crowded street. Meanwhile, Turner's focus on the labour of the sailors amid the destruction of the battle could be said to echo the armies of workers swarming over the scarred land of a brickfield.

Some responses to the painting were more positive. In 1858, *The Illustrated London News* declared that *The Battle of Trafalgar* had 'a thoroughly British and a thoroughly Jack-tarish character'. This comment highlighted the prominence of sailors within the painting, Jack Tar being a nickname for the seamen of the Royal Navy. The same review also included praise for Turner's depiction of ship-to-ship fighting, writing that, 'Nelson's flagship, with the memorable signal still flying, shows marks of rough usage, but her injuries are fearfully avenged upon the ships of the enemy, the rigging and spars of which are toppling down in all directions.' The critic's final verdict was that the picture was 'a graphic illustration of the maritime warfare of the past', since 'the like of Trafalgar' would never be seen again and future victories would 'differ materially in their characteristics from all that have gone before'.

When these words were written, more than half a century had elapsed since the Battle of Trafalgar. Massive technological shifts had occurred in that time, including the invention of steam power. The sailing ships of Nelson's fleet were now old-fashioned relics of an earlier era. The role of the Royal Navy had also changed. After defeating Napoleonic France in 1815, Britain was left with a vast empire and no major international rivals. Rather than fighting battles, British naval vessels were now primarily employed in survey work, peacekeeping and so-called 'gunboat diplomacy'. As the comments in *The Illustrated London News* demonstrate, these historical shifts affected attitudes towards Turner's painting. Viewers became less concerned about the factual inaccuracies that had enraged earlier commentators, instead regarding the picture through the lens of nostalgia.

The painting's rehabilitation also received support from art critic John Ruskin (1819–1900). As a teenager in the 1830s, Ruskin had developed a deep admiration for Turner's work. The following decade, he began writing in defence of his hero's artistic reputation. His most famous work was *Modern Painters*, a five-volume text published between 1843 and 1860. In his writings, Ruskin highlighted the importance of naval and maritime subjects within Turner's career, declaring that 'of all accessories to landscape, ships were throughout his life those which he studied with the greatest care'. While he acknowledged that Turner often took liberties with nautical details, he insisted that this elevated his paintings above those of artists who cleaved to the facts. Ruskin justified this claim by arguing that, although a warship is itself a work of art, 'art which reduplicates art is necessarily second-rate'. This opinion is unfair on more traditional marine painters, who were exceptionally skilled in their own way, but Ruskin was a partial critic, who regarded Turner as superior to all other artists.

In the fifth volume of *Modern Painters*, Ruskin asserted that Turner had represented the Battle of Trafalgar three times: 'once [...] for its death; twice [...] for its victory; thrice, in pensive farewell to the old *Temeraire*'. This comment referred to three paintings spread across the artist's career. *The Battle of Trafalgar* was the middle picture of the trio, being Turner's attempt to encapsulate the British fleet's victory in a single image. The first, meanwhile, was *The Battle of Trafalgar, as Seen from the Mizen Starboard Shrouds of the 'Victory'*, which showed the moment of Nelson's fatal wounding (or 'death', in Ruskin's words).

The third painting was *The Fighting Temeraire*, which Turner exhibited at the Royal Academy in 1839 (fig. 32). This picture shows a steam tug towing a wooden warship along the Thames to a scrapyard at Rotherhithe in the golden light of the setting sun. The condemned vessel is the *Temeraire*, which had fought three decades earlier at Trafalgar. Turner's inclusion of the word 'fighting' in his title alluded specifically

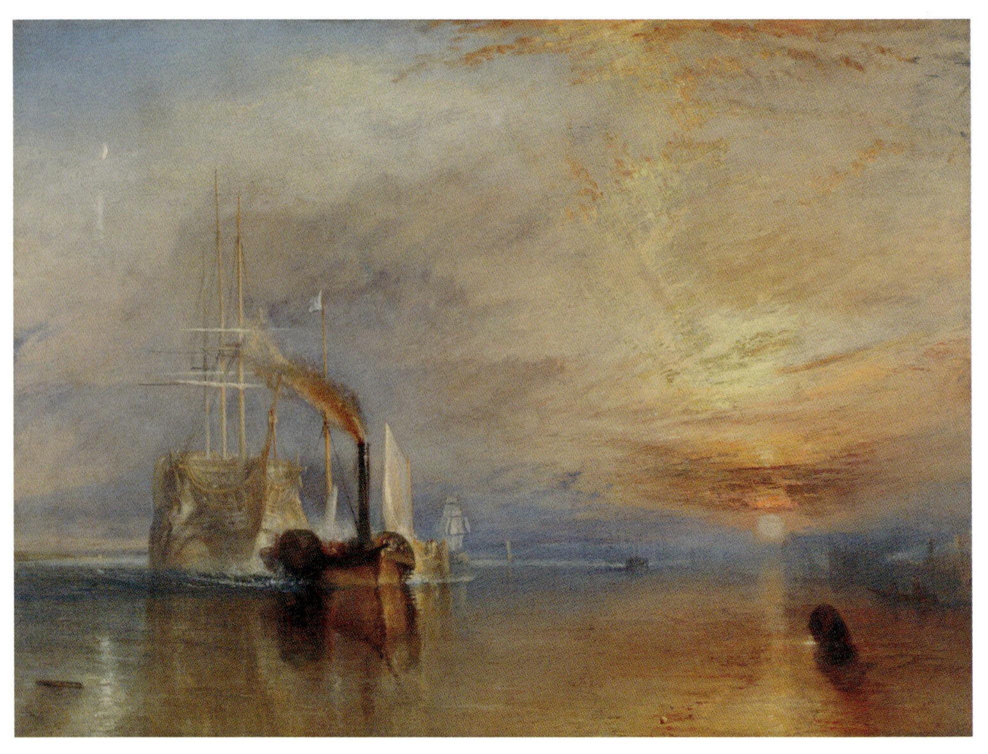

FIG. 32
The Fighting Temeraire,
J.M.W. Turner,
1839,
oil on canvas,
907 × 1,216mm,
The National Gallery,
London

to the ship's participation in the battle. Much like *The Battle of Trafalgar*, the painting deviates from historical fact. In reality, the *Temeraire* was a hulk without masts and rigging when it was towed to its final berth, but Turner imaginatively restored the lost features to evoke the ship's former glory. The painting as a whole is usually understood as an allegory of the passage of time, marking the technological transition from sail to steam and inviting nostalgia for past naval triumphs after several decades of peace.

The sentiments expressed in *The Fighting Temeraire* resonated with Ruskin. He belonged to a generation born after Trafalgar, for whom the battle seemed like part of a bygone age. He wrote of the need to preserve its memory, both by coaxing 'all current stories out of the wounded sailors' and by vowing that: 'Trafalgar shall have its tribute of memory.' This tribute was accomplished, Ruskin argued, in Turner's trilogy. His comments are typical of responses to *The Battle of Trafalgar* in the mid-nineteenth century. By that time, the painting hung in the National Gallery of Naval Art at Greenwich and was often celebrated as an important memorial to Britain's naval heritage.

The Naval Gallery

Some art historians have suggested that King George IV had *The Battle of Trafalgar* transferred from St James's Palace to Greenwich Hospital because he was embarrassed by the criticism that had been directed at the painting. However, another possibility is that, rather than expressing the King's disapproval, the relocation of the picture actually signalled his continued support for a major public museum, which he had championed since its foundation.

Commonly known as the Naval Gallery, the National Gallery of Naval Art opened in the Painted Hall at Greenwich Hospital in April 1824. Designed to provide a visual history of British maritime activity, its collection consisted of portraits, battle paintings and sculpture, alongside ship models, uniforms and naval equipment. Opening a few weeks prior to the foundation of the National Gallery in London, the Naval Gallery was the first public art gallery in Britain to describe itself as a 'national' institution.

Greenwich Hospital, where the gallery was situated, was a grand architectural complex on the banks of the River Thames, built on the site of a former royal palace. Established by Queen Mary II in 1695, the Hospital provided care and accommodation for elderly and disabled naval veterans. One of its most famous

FIG. 33
The Painted Hall,
Old Royal Naval College
(formerly Greenwich Hospital),
Greenwich,
2023

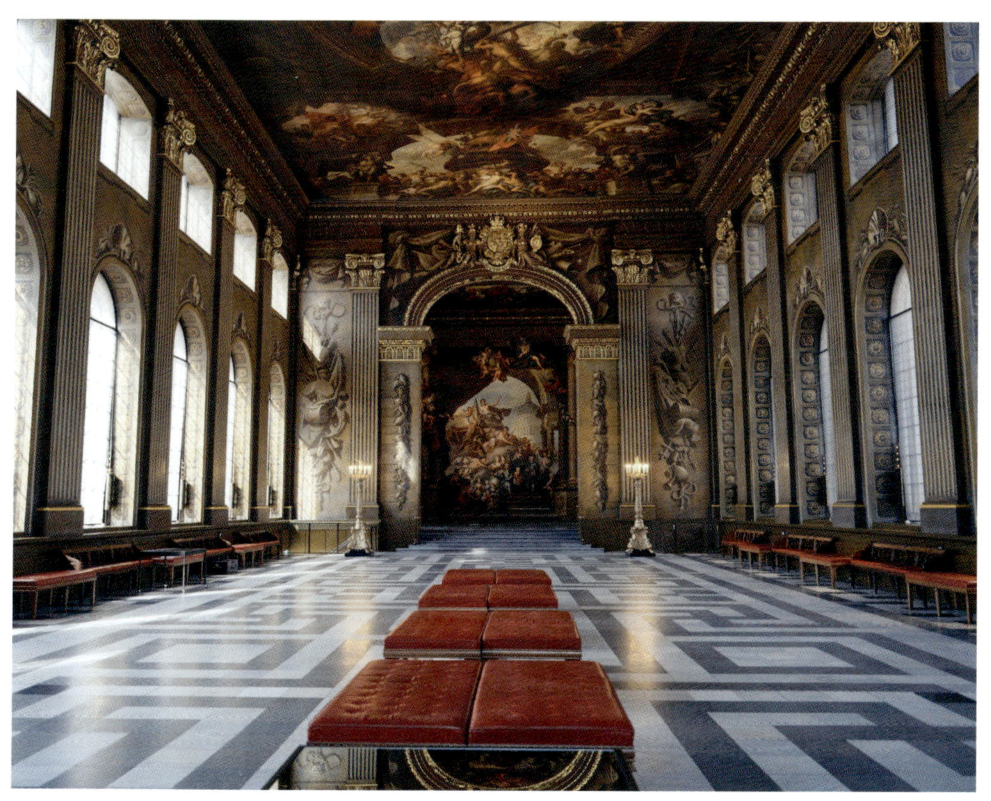

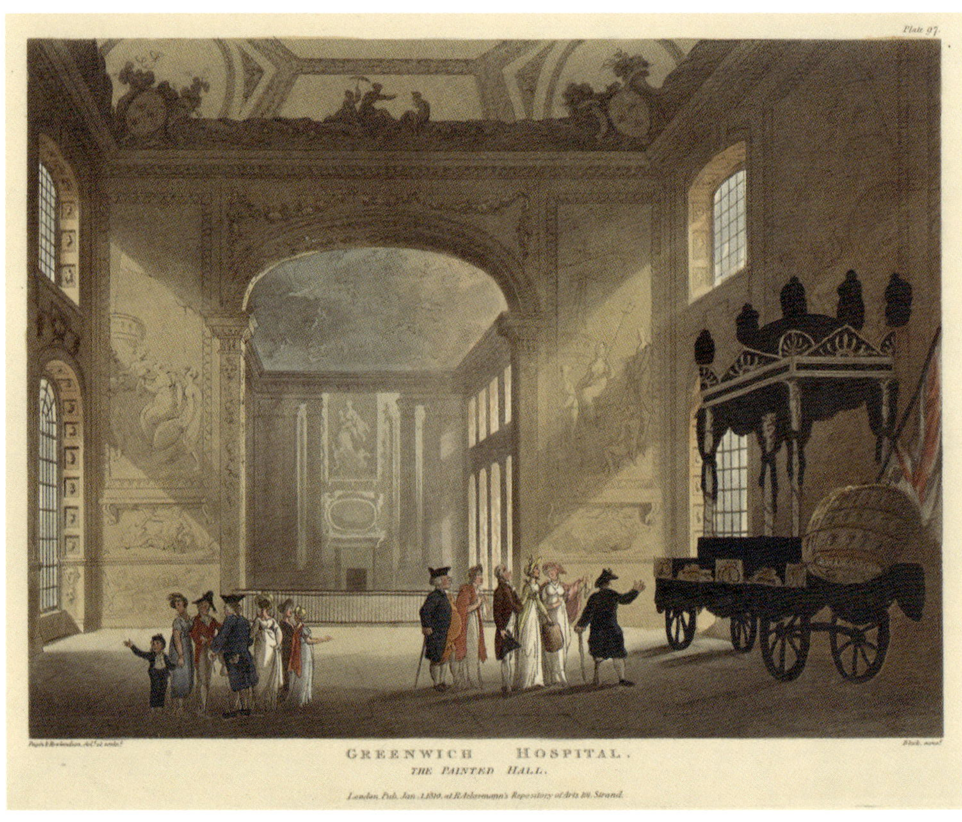

FIG. 34
Greenwich Hospital.
The Painted Hall,
John Bluck after Thomas Rowlandson and Augustus Charles Pugin, 1810,
aquatint on paper,
280 × 333mm,
PAF7631

rooms was the Painted Hall, which was originally built as a refectory but quickly became a tourist attraction, thanks to the spectacular murals that covered its walls and ceiling (fig. 33). Painted by James Thornhill between 1707 and 1726, the murals celebrated royal authority and naval triumph.

The idea of turning the Painted Hall into a gallery of maritime art was first suggested in 1795 by William Locker (1731–1800), a lieutenant-governor at the Hospital. Although Locker's plan failed to win support at the time, it was later revived by his son, Edward Hawke Locker (1777–1849), leading to the foundation of the Naval Gallery in 1824. In the intervening decades, the Painted Hall had been used for the lying-in-state of Nelson's body, prior to his burial at St Paul's Cathedral in January 1806. After the funeral, the carriage that had transported Nelson's coffin was placed on public display in the Hall, where it remained for over a decade. In 1810, it featured in Rudolf Ackermann's *Microcosm of London*, a collection of prints depicting famous locations around the city (fig. 34). The display of the funeral carriage was popular with visitors and established the Painted Hall as an important venue for the preservation of maritime history.

Locker recruited several high-profile individuals to help facilitate the development of the Naval Gallery. They included the President of the Royal Academy, Thomas Lawrence, who recommended alterations to the physical fabric of the Painted Hall to create more display space for paintings, and the politician and connoisseur Charles Long (1760–1838), who used his influential connections to help acquire artworks. Since the Directors of Greenwich Hospital did not want to divert funds away from its charitable work to purchase artworks for the new displays, Locker was reliant upon private donations to build the Naval Gallery's collection. Fortunately, Long was a royal advisor on artistic matters and convinced George IV to lend his support. The King made his first donation to the gallery in 1824, presenting a gift of 34 portraits of naval commanders from the royal collection. His generosity set a prestigious precedent, inspiring other art collectors and naval families to part with their own treasures.

As the collection grew, Locker compiled a wish list of officers and battles that he wanted to be represented in the Naval Gallery's displays. He sought to chart British naval success through the centuries, beginning with the defeat of the Spanish Armada in 1588 and culminating in the triumphs of the Napoleonic Wars. It was against this backdrop that George IV decided to reaffirm his support for the gallery with another donation. In 1829, he gave two major battle pictures, Turner's *Battle of Trafalgar* and De Loutherbourg's *Battle of the Glorious First of June*.

The Turner and the De Loutherbourg were initially displayed in the easternmost section of the Painted Hall. Known at the time as the Vestibule, this was the first space that visitors encountered. It served as a prologue to the main part of the gallery, which was accessed via a short staircase. In the Main Hall, the paintings were arranged by date, from earliest to most recent. However, the Vestibule was not included in this chronological arrangement. Instead, it focused on the Revolutionary and Napoleonic Wars, presenting these recent conflicts as the apogee of British naval achievement.

The appearance of the Vestibule was recorded by the artist John Scarlett Davis (1804–45) in 1830 (fig. 35). In Davis's painting, *The Battle of Trafalgar* can be seen on the right, hanging opposite *The Battle of the Glorious First of June*. The two paintings dominate the space, creating a spectacular first impression for visitors entering the Naval Gallery. Also displayed are a small number of eighteenth-century naval portraits and two plaster casts of life-size sculptures depicting celebrated naval commanders. One is of Nelson, appropriately positioned beside Turner's painting of his final victory. The other represents Admiral Adam Duncan (1731–1804), whose fleet defeated the Dutch at the Battle of Camperdown on 11 October 1797. Both casts, as well as two not shown in Davis's painting, were made for the Naval Gallery from the

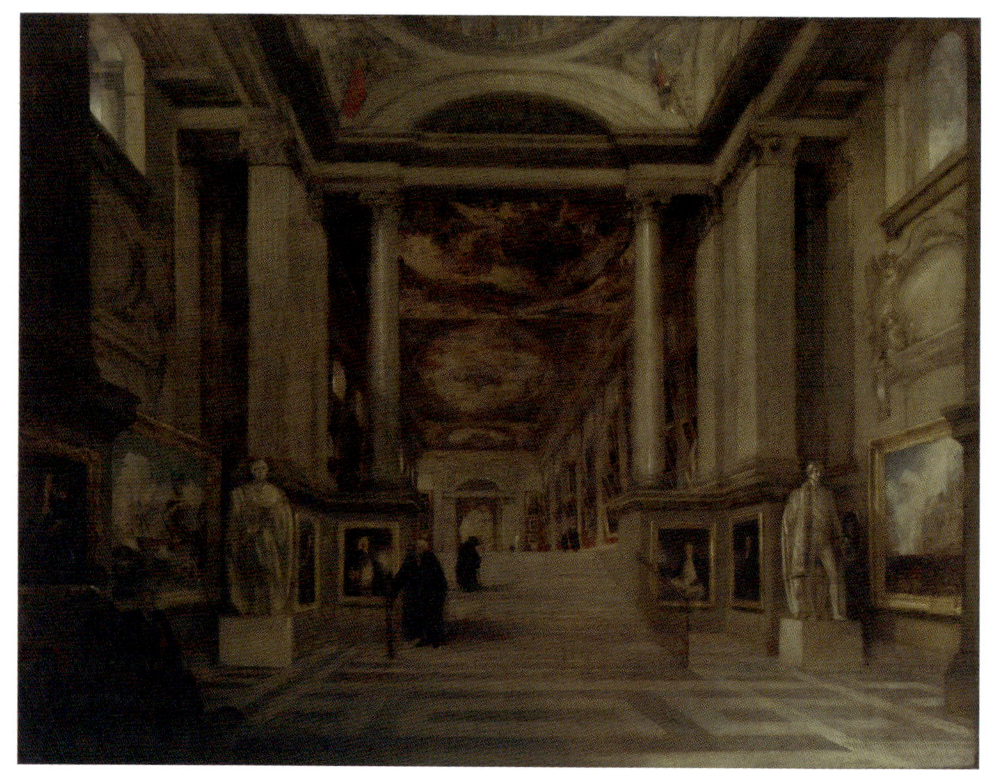

FIG. 35
The Painted Hall, Greenwich, John Scarlett Davis, 1830, oil on canvas, 1,127 × 1,435mm, The Walters Art Museum, Baltimore

officers' government-funded monuments in St Paul's Cathedral, linking the displays in the Painted Hall to another important site of national commemoration.

The Battle of Trafalgar remained on display in the Vestibule until the mid-1840s, when it moved to the main part of the gallery. This relocation was part of a reorganisation overseen by the marine painter Clarkson Stanfield (1793–1867), who took charge of the Naval Gallery after Locker retired in 1844. Stanfield inherited a collection that was fast outgrowing the existing display space. To solve this problem, he expanded the displays into an old storeroom adjoining the Painted Hall. This became the Nelson Room, a repository for art and artefacts relating to the famous admiral. Meanwhile, panelling was erected over the pilasters that broke up the walls of the Main Hall, creating more space for paintings. Upon this new surface, Stanfield hung the pictures in a dense configuration, their frames butting up against one and another. He also abandoned Locker's insistence on chronological order, mixing together artworks from different periods.

The new arrangement of the Main Hall was sketched for *The Illustrated London News* by Lemon Hart Michael (1824–1902) in 1865 (fig. 36). A subsequent iteration of the display is also recorded in a late nineteenth-century photograph (fig. 37). As these images show, De Loutherbourg's *Battle of the*

FIG. 36
View of the Naval Gallery in the Painted Hall, Greenwich Hospital, Lemon Hart Michael, 1865, watercolour on paper, 342 × 505mm, PAH4034

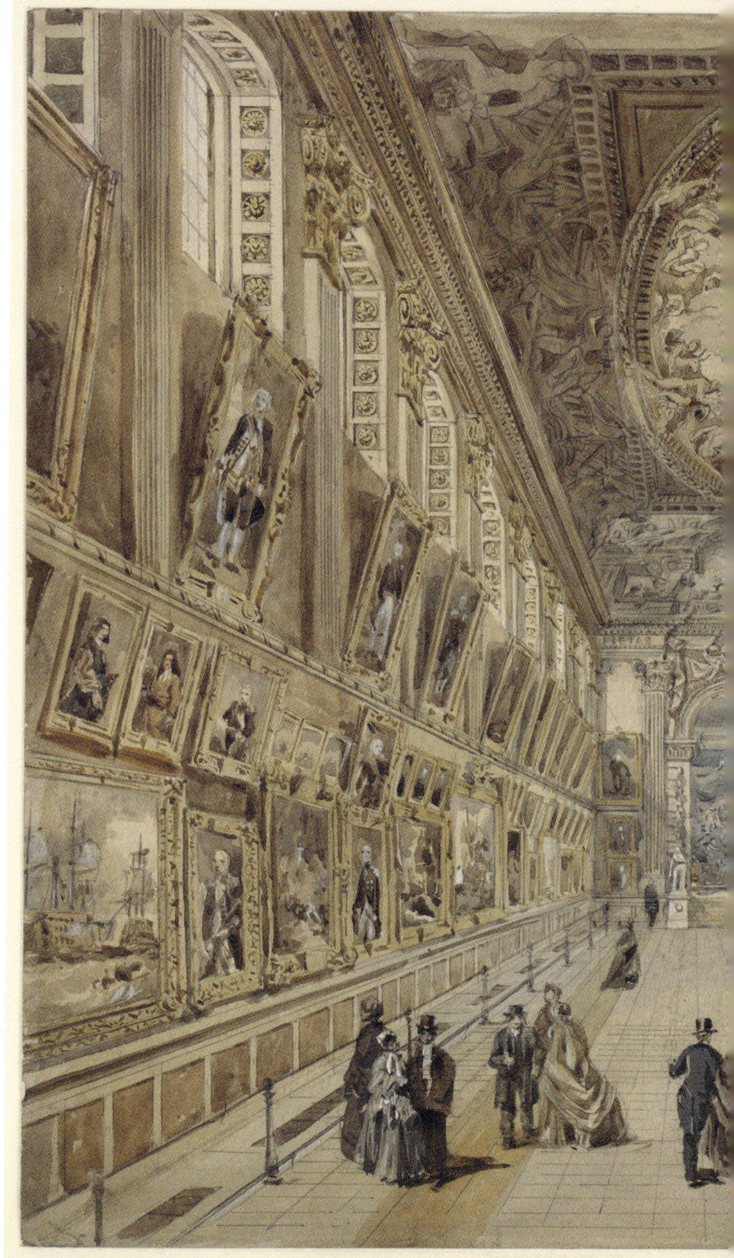

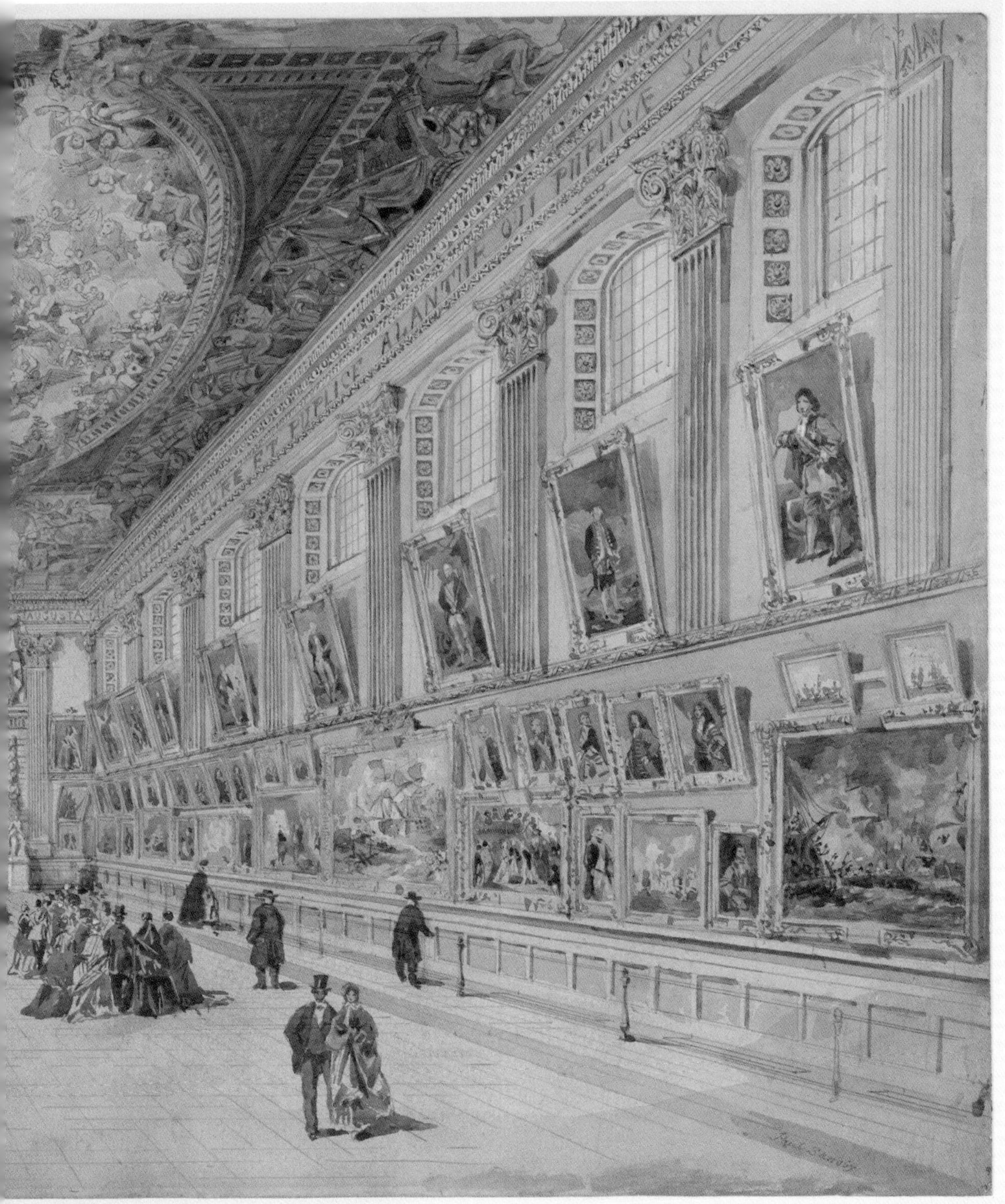

FIG. 37
Painted Hall of Greenwich Hospital (from Upper Hall), unknown photographer, late nineteenth century, photographic print, F7667

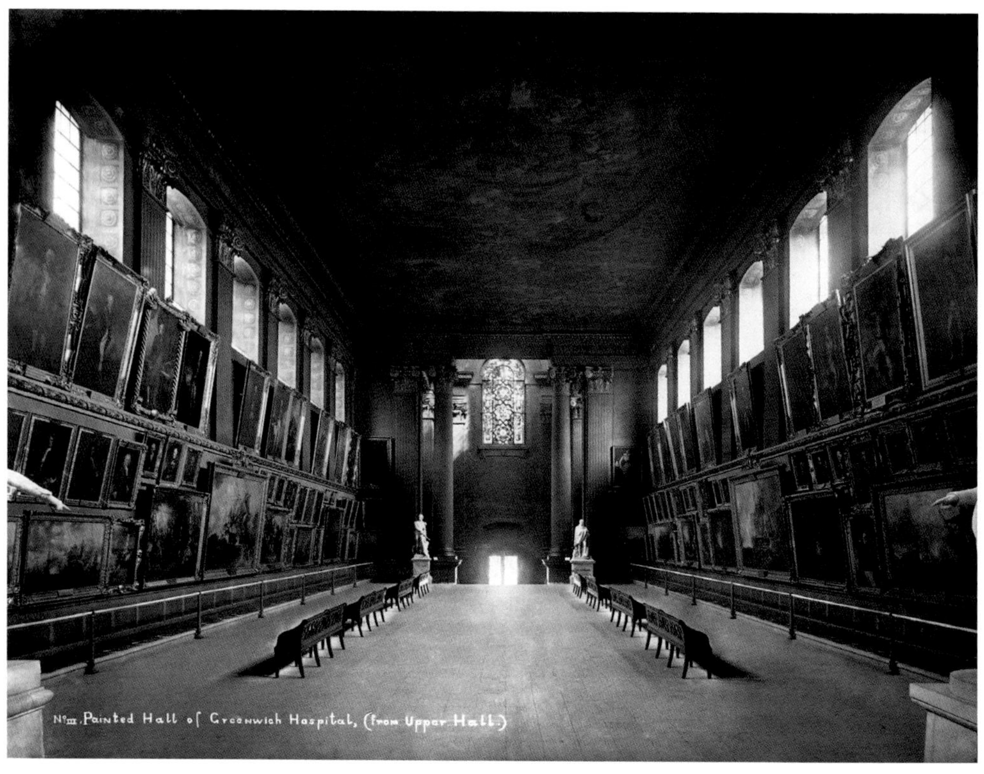

Glorious First of June and Turner's *Battle of Trafalgar* hung at the centre of the north and south walls respectively, facing each other across the room as they had previously done in the Vestibule. The two pictures were now the centrepieces of the gallery.

Art critics and travel writers often remarked that Greenwich Hospital was a fitting home for the Naval Gallery because of its history as a refuge for retired and injured sailors. As Francis Huskisson wrote in *The Art Journal* in 1889, 'There hundreds of the veterans who had fought and bled under the commanders whose deeds are represented, or whose features are preserved to posterity by pictures in the Hall, spent their last days.' This context was especially appropriate for *The Battle of Trafalgar*, emphasising as it did the labour and suffering of common sailors. Some Greenwich Pensioners may well have identified with the figures battling for survival in the foreground of the picture.

Pensioners continued to live on site at Greenwich Hospital until 1869, and many were employed as wardens and tour guides at the Naval Gallery. As well as talking about the artwork on display, they shared memories from their own careers with visitors. Their colourful tales of naval life became an important part of the gallery's public appeal, as shown in a series of watercolour sketches by the artist John Burnet (1784–1868),

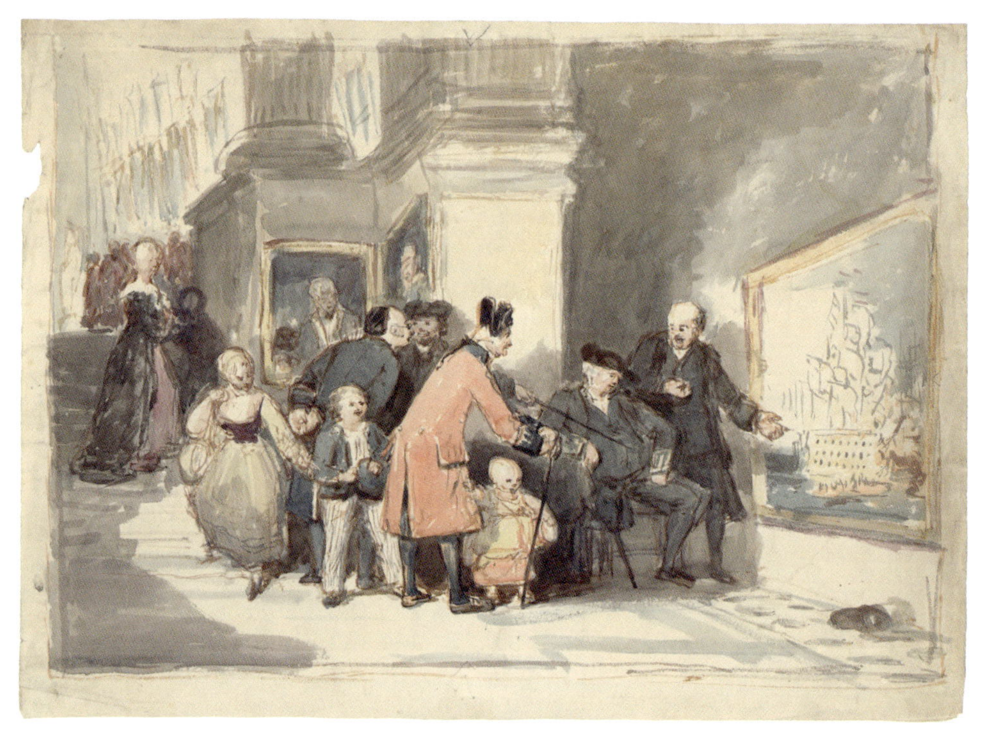

FIG. 38
Sketch for
'A Tale of Trafalgar',
John Burnet,
after 1829,
watercolour on paper,
445 × 595mm,
PAH3983

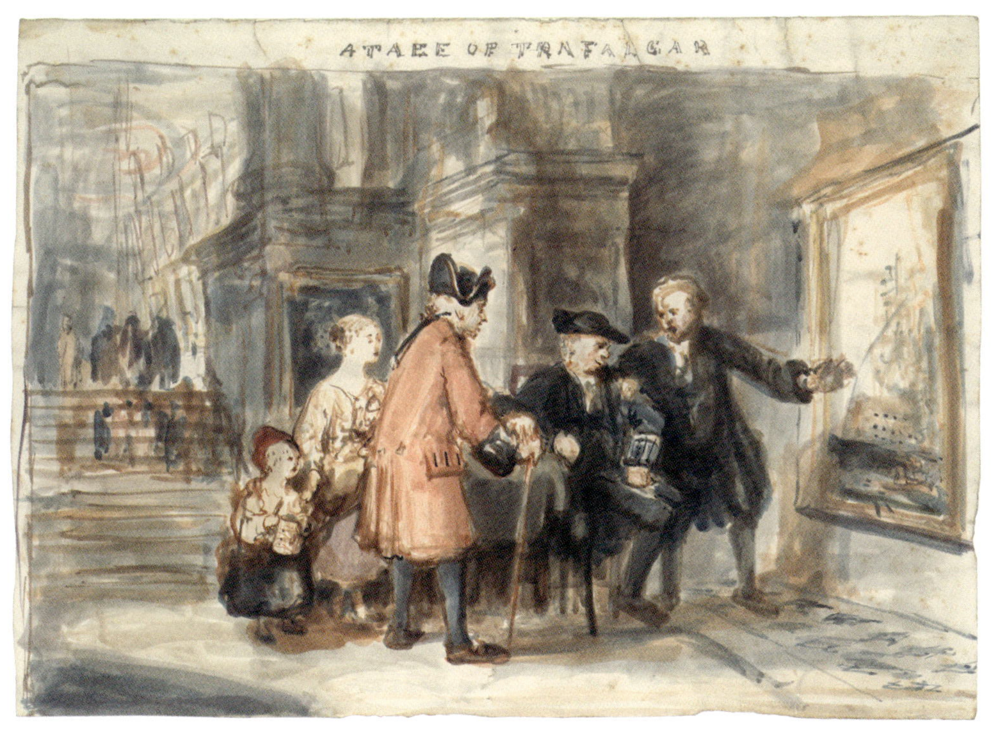

FIG. 39
Sketch for
'A Tale of Trafalgar',
John Burnet,
after 1829,
watercolour on paper,
361 × 495mm,
PAH3984

probably dating from the 1830s (figs 38 and 39). These sketches appear to be preparatory studies for a larger painting, which is either now lost or was never executed. The Greenwich Pensioners are distinguished by their blue uniforms. Several have walking sticks, and one has a wooden prosthesis, presumably having lost his leg in battle. They gesture at *The Battle of Trafalgar*, while a small crowd gathers around to hear their observations, including women, children and a man in a red coat. He is a military pensioner from the Royal Hospital at Chelsea, who has apparently come to swap war stories with his naval counterparts. The scene is designed to be patriotic and nostalgic. It celebrates the transmission of British naval heritage to future generations via both Turner's painting and the words of the ageing veterans. It is significant that, of all the artworks in the Painted Hall, Burnet selected *The Battle of Trafalgar* as the focal point for his image. His choice demonstrates that Turner's picture was one of the most celebrated and recognisable paintings in the Naval Gallery.

At Greenwich, *The Battle of Trafalgar* had found a prestigious and high-profile home. Throughout the nineteenth century, the Naval Gallery attracted a large number of visitors, although the institution was often ignored by the art world. To quote a review published in the literary magazine *The Athenaeum* in July 1870:

> There is no public collection of pictures which is less visited by artists and archaeological students than that in the Painted Hall of Greenwich Hospital. On the other hand, there is scarcely one that is more popular.

The Naval Gallery eventually closed in 1936, but that was not the end for its collection, which was transferred on long-term loan to the brand new National Maritime Museum, situated just across the road from the Painted Hall. Turner's painting thus became a foundational artwork within the Museum's collection, and it remains one of its highlights to this day.

Since its unveiling in St James's Palace more than 200 years ago, *The Battle of Trafalgar* has been dogged by criticism. However, while the picture may have its flaws, its significance can be measured in other ways. It is one of Turner's largest and most complex paintings, commemorating a naval battle which had acquired legendary status in the British cultural imagination. It memorialises not only the Royal Navy's victory and the loss of Nelson but also the suffering of common sailors. And, although it was ejected from the royal collection, its transfer to a national art gallery ensured that it became a well-known and popular artwork among the British public.

Further Reading

Turner

Barrie, David (ed.), *John Ruskin: Modern Painters*, Pilkington Press, London, 2005

Butlin, Martin and Evelyn Joll, *The Paintings of J.M.W. Turner*, 2 vols, rev. edn., Yale University Press, New Haven/London, 1984

Moyle, Franny, *The Extraordinary Life and Momentous Times of J.M.W. Turner*, Viking, London, 2016

Riding, Christine and Richard Johns (eds), *Turner & the Sea*, Thames & Hudson, London, 2013

Trafalgar, Nelson and the Royal Navy

Adkins, Roy, *Nelson's Trafalgar: The Battle That Changed the World*, Penguin, London, 2006

Clayton, Tim, *Tars: The Men who Made Britain Rule the Waves*, Hodder & Stoughton, London, 2007

Costello, Ray, *Black Salt: Seafarers of African Descent on British Ships*, Liverpool University Press, Liverpool, 2012

Lambert, Andrew, *Nelson: Britannia's God of War*, Faber & Faber, London, 2005

Rodger, N.A.M., *The Command of the Ocean: A Naval History of Britain, 1649–1815*, Penguin, London, 2004

Greenwich

Quilley, Geoff (ed.), *Art for the Nation: The Oil Paintings Collections of the National Maritime Museum*, National Maritime Museum, London, 2006

Acknowledgements | Picture Credits

Many thanks to Kathleen Bloomfield and the Publishing Team for the opportunity to write this book. Louise Jarrold has been an excellent editor, and I am grateful to the Museum's Photo Studio for producing the detailed images of the painting.

Every attempt has been made to trace accurate ownership of copyrighted images in this book. Any errors or omissions will be corrected in subsequent editions provided notification is sent to the publisher. Unless otherwise stated, images are © National Maritime Museum, Greenwich, London.

Cover and various internal pages: © National Maritime Museum, Greenwich, London, Greenwich Hospital Collection

p. 10 Tate, purchased 1972. Photo: Tate
p. 15 Tate, accepted by the nation as part of the Turner Bequest 1856. Photo: Tate
p. 22 © National Museums Liverpool / Bridgeman Images
pp. 24–25 © National Maritime Museum, Greenwich, London, Greenwich Hospital Collection
p. 28 Tate, bequeathed by Henry Vaughan 1900. Photo: Tate
pp. 30–31 Tate, accepted by the nation as part of the Turner Bequest 1856. Photo: Tate
pp. 34–35 © National Maritime Museum, Greenwich, London, Greenwich Hospital Collection
pp. 36–37 © Crown copyright. National Maritime Museum, Greenwich, London
p. 42 Tate, accepted by the nation as part of the Turner Bequest 1856. Photo: Tate
p. 43 Tate, accepted by the nation as part of the Turner Bequest 1856. Photo: Tate
p. 60 Tate, accepted by the nation as part of the Turner Bequest 1856. Photo: Tate
p. 67 Photograph © 2025, Museum of Fine Arts, Boston. Henry Lillie Pierce Fund
p. 70 © Royal Collection Enterprises Limited 2024 | Royal Collection Trust
p. 76 © The National Gallery, London. All rights reserved
p. 79 Painted Hall, 2023, Hugh Fox. © Hugh Fox. Photo: Old Royal Naval College.
p. 84 The Walters Art Museum. Acquired by Henry Walters

First published in 2025 by Royal Museums Greenwich
Park Row, Greenwich, London, SE10 9NF

publishing@rmg.co.uk

ISBN: 978-1-0687659-9-5

At the heart of the UNESCO World Heritage Site of Maritime Greenwich are the four world-class attractions of Royal Museums Greenwich – the National Maritime Museum, the Royal Observatory, the Queen's House and *Cutty Sark*.

rmg.co.uk

 A CIP catalogue record for this book is available from the British Library.

Design by Peter Dawson, Ronja Rønning, www.gradedesign.com
Printed and bound by Green Leaf Production, Slovenia

10 9 8 7 6 5 4 3 2 1